Raising Faith

A True Story of Raising a Child Psychic-Medium

T0127495

Raising
Faith

A True Story of Raising a Child
Psychic-Medium

Claire Waters

Winchester, UK
Washington, USA

First published by Sixth Books, 2019
Sixth Books is an imprint of John Hunt Publishing Ltd., No. 3 East St., Alresford,
Hampshire SO24 9EE, UK
office1@jhpbooks.net
www.johnhuntpublishing.com
www.6th-books.com

For distributor details and how to order please visit the 'Ordering' section on our website.

ISBN: 978 1 78535 870 8
978 1 78535 871 5 (ebook)
Library of Congress Control Number: 2017957394

A CIP catalogue record for this book is available from the British Library.

Design: Stuart Davies

Printed and bound by CPI Group (UK) Ltd, Croydon, CR0 4YY, UK

We operate a distinctive and ethical publishing philosophy in
all areas of our business, from our global network of authors to
production and worldwide distribution.

Contents

FOREWORD   1

BEFORE WE BEGIN   2
COURAGE   4
TURNING POINT   9
ASKING FAITH   20
THE LITTLE GIRL   24
THE NURSE   29
SPIRITUAL CHURCH   33
PAUL   39
SHARING OUR SECRET   42
GREAT GRANDDAD   47
GREAT-NAN IS FLYING   51
JOURNEY OF SPIRITUAL DEVELOPMENT   53
    Auras   54
    Trust Your Own Instincts   56
    Spiritual Workshops   57
    Gift of Touch   60
SPIRIT GUIDES   62
WILL   65
TSUNAMI   67
BOBBY   69
COINCIDENCES   71
COMMUNICATING WITH SPIRIT   75
FAITH'S PERSPECTIVE   78
FAVOURITE DAY OUT   83
    Frightening Visions   84
SENSITIVE TO OUR ENVIRONMENT   86
    Protecting Our Energy   87
    Are there 'Bad' Spirits?   93
    Food Sensitivities   97

GEMS OF WISDOM   99
  Life Lessons   99
  When One Door Closes...   101
  The Law of Attraction   102
  Life After Death   103
  The Gift of Psychic-Mediumship   105
THE JOURNEY SO FAR   107

RECOMMENDED READING   108

FOREWORD

With the growing number of psychic children being born into the world, there is a need for genuine support and guidance for parents navigating this subject for the first time. Learning your child has psychic abilities can be a daunting revelation, but Raising Faith details one family's discovery of their daughter's spiritual gifts, their journey to understand about the spirit world, and how to balance spiritual gifts with everyday parenting challenges.

This book is a valuable and much needed support to anyone raising psychic children, or wanting to learn more about our loved ones and spirit guides who continue to help and support us from the spirit world.

Stewart Keeys, Celebrity Psychic Medium

BEFORE WE BEGIN

When our daughter Faith was four years old, we discovered she was a Psychic-Medium. That is, she could see, hear, feel and communicate with people who had died. Faith is now twelve years old, and her ability to communicate with these 'spirit people' is as strong today as it has ever been. Raising a child with psychic gifts adds a layer of complexity to parenting which has required an open mind, a willingness to learn, and a respectful acceptance that everything we see, hear or have been raised to believe, isn't necessarily all that exists in this incredible universe.

The journey we have been on together as a mother, daughter and family has been extraordinary. In the beginning, we knew very little about psychic and spiritual matters but, during the past eight years, we have been privileged to communicate with spirit people every day, including regular visits and conversations with our loved ones who have passed, and receiving guidance from our spirit helpers and guides both in times of difficulty and to help confirm or clarify my own understanding of the spirit world.

My desire to understand my young daughter's experiences inspired me to learn as much as I could about this subject. My learning journey became much more than I ever expected. The spiritual laws and understandings that I have acquired are life changing, both for me and for anyone wishing to understand more about life here and now, and life after death of the physical body.

I feel incredibly proud and blessed to share this journey with Faith. How she lives her life as a 'normal' young girl alongside her psychic-medium abilities is inspirational, but it's not always easy. *Raising Faith* details the many challenges we have experienced as part of our journey together, including helping

Faith manage the messages she receives from spirit, learning how to create boundaries with the spirits who visit her, responding with integrity to the messages and guidance we receive, learning how to protect our energy, and how to encourage only positive spirits and messages around us. We have learned the hard way that negative darker energies can be attracted to us, and have learned how to prevent and detach these. We have discovered that the health and emotional well-being of sensitive, empathic and psychic people can be easily affected by the places we visit, the people we spend time with, and the foods (even healthy foods!) that we consume.

If this book has found its way into your hands, know that there is a good reason for that. I hope that the contents within helps answer your questions, brings you comfort, knowledge, and inspiration and helps you progress forwards on your own life journey.

If you have lost loved ones, know that they are still with you, loving you, watching over you, encouraging you to move forwards and to live your life for your highest good.

Raising sensitive, empathic and psychic children can leave parents, guardians and their families feeling overwhelmed and isolated at times. The challenges are numerous, yet despite the growing number of these extraordinary children coming into the world, the information and support available to help their families is extremely limited. If your family is blessed with psychic abilities, I hope this book helps you feel comforted to know that you are not alone.

Claire Waters

COURAGE

It was bedtime and I had not long finished reading Faith a story. She was lying on her back, snuggled under the covers, quietly staring towards the end of her bed. This was the time of day in our house when our lives became a combination of the perfectly ordinary, interspersed with extraordinary moments.

As with most other young children, bedtimes for Faith began with a bath and cleaning her teeth, followed by jumping into bed for a story, and sometimes a conversation about her day, or the fun we had planned for tomorrow.

It was at these times when she was settled in bed, quiet and comfortable, that Faith was most likely to talk about the spirit people that she could see around her.

On this occasion, some months after we had first learned of Faith's psychic abilities, I sat quietly watching as she lay there. She continued to stare straight ahead, relaxed but concentrating on something. My gaze followed to where she was staring, but all I could see were her pink gingham bedroom curtains.

I took a deep breath as I waited. These experiences, as amazing as I found them, still unnerved me. I knew so little about this subject, and although I was trying to learn as much as I could, I was still uncomfortable with the idea that people were around me and my daughter could communicate with them, yet I couldn't see them.

I spoke as calm and confidently as I could, belying the nerves I felt inside. "What can you see?" I asked her quietly.

"It's a new man!" she said with surprise. Her face lit up as she told me, but she continued staring straight ahead, watching and listening to him.

I smiled, trying to hide my true feelings, but inside my fears were running rampant. Usually our spirit visitors were familiar to Faith, so who was this 'new' man my daughter could see? Was he friend or foe? I felt vulnerable and out of my depth. As her mother I should have known more than she did so I could help protect her, but on this subject, Faith was more knowledgeable than I was. For as long as she could remember, there were spirit people who had helped and protected her.

Hiding my unease I asked, "What does he look like?"

She continued to watch him. "He looks a bit like Abby's Daddy." I pictured the man I'd seen on the school playground who had short, blond wavy hair and a dusting of freckles across his face.

I hesitated for a few moments whilst I thought about who this man could be. I watched Faith, who was usually very shy, as she lay looking calm and comfortable, even with this strange man in her bedroom. I had always relied a lot on instincts during my life, and despite my concerns about this new visitor, my instincts told me not to be alarmed, so we continued.

I took another deep breath. "Why is he here?" I asked, and waited anxiously for her answer.

She concentrated for a few moments, and then said, "He says he's come to help me with courage."

I thought about this for a moment, and then smiled as I realized the reason for his visit. I had recently learned about spirit guides who visited us to help in times of need, and I suspected this was why he had come.

"Is this man one of your guides?" I asked Faith.

She then repeated what the man was telling her. "Yes."

"I thought so. How lovely. He's come to help you feel brave at school," I explained.

Faith had recently started school, and was learning to cope with some strong characters within her class. There had been some friendship issues which she had been worried about, so, during the past few days, we had been talking about this. Whilst 'courage' might have seemed a suitable word within the conversation, this word was not part of Faith's vocabulary at only five years old.

"Why don't you ask him who he is?" I encouraged. I was eager to hear more about this man, now that I felt more confident about the reason for his visit.

She lay quietly concentrating again on the end of the bed. "He says his name was Joseph Frederickson."

Frederickson wasn't a name I was familiar with at all. It occurred to me that perhaps this visitor wasn't from England. "Did he live in England?" I asked her.

"Yes," she answered immediately.

"Which town or county did he live in?" I was silently wondering if I could find any historical information or evidence about him.

Faith paused as she listened to him. "Somewhere in the middle, it begins with an M. He can't tell us any more about that."

I nodded respectfully, as I felt perhaps I shouldn't be trying to find 'evidence' to prove this man's identity. Perhaps that was an inappropriate way to use Faith's gift.

"Can he tell us anything else about himself?" I prompted.

Faith was watching and listening carefully. I was expecting her to tell me his age, or where he lived, or something warm and reassuring, but instead she told me, "He was killed in a car crash."

I was shocked and speechless for a few moments. I wasn't expecting to hear how he died. My thoughts were jumping ahead to where this conversation could lead, and how unsuitable this might be for my young daughter to hear. It had never occurred to me that perhaps we might be told frightening details. Talking about dying in such a dramatic and potentially violent way was not a subject I considered suitable for my young daughter to be involved in.

I fidgeted uncomfortably as I mulled over what to do next. Despite my shock and concern at the answer provided, Faith still wasn't frightened at all, either by the man or by the conversation. She was very calm and matter-of-fact about the information she was apparently being told.

I had learned from Faith that we don't have to speak outwardly to spirit for them to hear us, so I silently 'asked' for nothing frightening to be mentioned.

Hesitantly, we continued as if this was a perfectly normal bedtime conversation. "That's very sad. Can he tell us anything else?"

"He had two children. A boy and a girl."

"How old were his children?"

She frowned as she concentrated on listening. "He says they were sixteen and twenty-one when he died. He still visits them all the time."

I nodded my head in understanding as I mulled over what the man had told her.

"So, next time you are worried at school, you can call Joseph and he will help you feel brave." I smiled to reassure her. "How lovely that you have all these people to help you."

Faith was sleepy now. I tucked her covers around her again as she settled down to sleep, kissed her goodnight and quietly left her room. As I began to close the door, I questioned whether I should leave my daughter to sleep in her bedroom by herself, knowing the spirit man may still be with her. I would have been frightened to sleep in her room after that experience, but she was perfectly at ease and comfortable with these visits. For my own peace of mind, instead of closing the door behind me fully, I left it ajar. I stood outside her room for a few moments, shaking my head in amazement at the conversation we had just had.

On many nights we have similar experiences. Usually, it's the same familiar spirit people who visit, many of whom are deceased family members, and most of whom died before Faith was born. Other times, as on this occasion, a new spirit person visits us, usually to help with a specific situation we are experiencing.

This has become our version of 'ordinary' since discovering our daughter is a psychic-medium.

TURNING POINT

Earlier in my life, I had given little thought to what happens to us after death, however, the following experience helped shape the beliefs I have today.

When my children were very young, and some months before the conversation I had with Faith about Joseph Frederickson, my mother had popped around to our house for a cup of tea. As she was leaving, I stood in the open doorway watching her walk down the driveway back to her car. She stopped just before she climbed in, and turned to look at me. "I've just remembered. I've left a book for you to read," she said. "I think you might like it."

"Okay, I'll have a look," I answered non-committedly.

As I was closing the front door I saw the book on the window ledge inside the porch. It had the title, *Many Lives, Many Masters* and was by Dr. Brian L. Weiss. I hadn't heard of it despite its popularity, but reading this book was to be a turning point in my life. The book was a true story about an American medical psychiatrist who, during hypnosis treatment on his patients, had inadvertently stumbled across past-life experiences which were affecting their present lives. This was a respectable medical doctor who had credibility and who was relatively skeptical about past-lives and reincarnation. That was until many repeat experiences with the past-life experiences of his patients had solidified his findings.

I had always been 'on the fence' so to speak about issues such as reincarnation even though I had always been interested in my mother's stories from her occasional visits to a psychic medium when I was in my teens. My childhood was relatively conservative, and subjects such as reincarnation and alternative therapies had never crossed my path before. It was in my late teens that I discovered homeopathic medicine and loved it so much that a few years later I began my training to become a professional homeopath. It had been during this training in London that the subject of reincarnation had first come up.

It was the first day of a four-year course and the participants all took a seat in the room where the class was being held. An attractive lady with a dark blonde bob and blue eyes walked towards me purposefully and took the seat next to mine and introduced herself as Karen. Later that day we were talking and I mentioned how I always enjoyed wartime movies and music. Her face lit up and she announced quite matter-of-factly, "Ah, that's why I was drawn to sit with you. We have known each other before in a past life."

I stared at her blankly, feeling uncomfortable and naive. Past life? I had no idea what she was talking about, and I wasn't sure how to respond to such a bizarre statement.

Before starting my homeopathy course, I had been teased by skeptical friends that I was likely to meet some alternative-minded 'hippy' people, but I hadn't really known what to expect. I was born and raised in rural Hampshire in the UK and my life had been relatively sheltered from liberal-minded influences. This lady didn't fit my ignorant expectations of an 'alternative-hippy type'. She was smartly dressed and groomed, a professional consultant in the city and couldn't have been farther from my stereotypical expectations. Fortunately, I kept my opinions to myself and we went on to become good friends.

Although I was not at that time open-minded enough to embrace her beliefs, as a Reiki master, Karen had been my first spiritual influence and a loyal confidante.

Having mulled over my bizarre conversation with Karen some years before, my curiosity was sparked and I finished reading the back cover of Dr. Weiss's book.

I found the book absolutely fascinating and finished reading it within a day or two. Eager to learn more, my thoughts drifted to Gareth, the hypnotherapist who worked at the clinic where I was the resident homeopath. I wondered if during his sessions with patients he had ever heard of past lives. I didn't know him well. We had only met in passing at the clinic, and at the annual Christmas dinner.

I telephoned him and told him about the book I had just finished reading. "Oh yes, often," was his answer when I asked him if he'd come across past lives. "I don't believe in it myself, but I do offer past-life regression sessions."

I was surprised by his comments. How could he offer and charge his clients for a professional service that he didn't believe in? It didn't make sense to me.

"One client's past-life regression during hypnosis had so much detail that I actually researched it, to validate the information," he continued. "During hypnosis, she'd provided her name and that of her then husband, the street where they lived, and that he was a doctor. I was able to trace the house she'd previously lived in and find out where the husband worked. It all matched surprisingly well with the information she'd given during her session. But I still don't believe it."

"Why not, when you'd validated so much of what she mentioned during her session?" I asked.

"I'm a very scientific person. I like data and statistical results. I need more evidence than that. I can't explain it."

"Do you believe in life after death?" I asked him.

"Not really, but one of my clients is a psychic-medium. I can put you in touch with her if you like. She can probably answer your questions."

I was unnerved at the idea of talking to a psychic lady, but took comfort in the fact Gareth knew her. I agreed that he could give her my phone number.

The next day, I received a phone call from this lady, Gloria. I awkwardly told her of the book I had read and how interesting I had found it. She kindly offered to meet with me to answer any questions I might have, and to discuss the subject further. I hesitated only slightly before inviting her to my home the next day.

I was nervous as I waited for Gloria to arrive. I had never met a psychic-medium before and I had no idea what to expect. At that time, my knowledge about psychics, mediums and all things spiritual was limited to the stories I'd heard in my teenage years when my mother had visited a psychic medium, following the passing of her father. I recalled my mother excitedly telling me some weeks after her reading with the psychic lady that she had booked an appointment for me too. I was quite indignant at the time that I didn't want a 'fortune telling' and I had insisted she cancel the appointment. I had always found the subject fascinating and terrifying in equal measures. I had assumed they would tell me something about my future that could potentially change the choices I made, and subsequently my path in life, and that hadn't seemed right to me. Interestingly, unlike many people, I had never been skeptical of their abilities, just fearful of them. Now, here I was, anxiously anticipating the arrival of a psychic to my own home! Would Gloria already know things about me? Would she be able to read my thoughts? Would she tell me something I didn't want to hear? What was I thinking? This had all started because I was curious to talk to someone about a book I found fascinating!

When Gloria arrived, the first thing I noticed were the dark circles beneath her eyes. She looked exhausted. She was a few years older than I was, with thick, shoulder length, curly, brown hair and serious dark brown eyes. I found out later she had many food intolerances and this was the cause of the dark circles.

It was an awkward start. She seemed as nervous as I was.

"This is one of the few times I've left my home in the last few months," she admitted. "I've been experiencing agoraphobia, so it was difficult for me to come here today."

I listened with interest as Gloria explained she'd had an incident some months earlier, which had left her in this state of fear, and she had since been reluctant to leave her home.

As nervous as she was, I found her an assertive and

intimidating character. I was curious to know what had happened to her, but my instincts told me to tread carefully. I didn't have the courage to ask, so, as I busied myself making us a cup of tea, Gloria explained how she had prepared herself for her visit to me. She had apparently seen my home in her mind and walked around it before she even arrived here. *Creepy!* I thought. *How is that possible?*

As we wandered into the sitting room and made ourselves comfortable on the sofas with a cup of tea each, she brought out a Tupperware box with biscuits that were safe for her to eat with her food intolerances. "Please help yourself," she offered, placing the box on the coffee table between us.

Gloria went on to explain that she managed her psychic-medium abilities alongside a 'normal' job. Weekdays she earned her living as a professional business consultant, and she was fortunate that she was mostly able to work from home. At the weekends, she was often asked to lead the services at spiritual churches in neighboring counties. In addition, she ran psychic development workshops independently.

I began talking about the book and Gloria confirmed everything I had read was true, according to her own experiences. I had so many questions for her, influenced by what I had read.

"Does everybody have past lives?" I asked.

"Yes." She nodded as she began answering. "We each have many. At the end of our life when our physical body dies, our soul returns to the spirit world. We then spend some time in spirit reflecting on the lessons we have learned in this lifetime. These lessons are merged with all the lessons we have learnt from our previous lifetimes. Each time we are born again, we come to learn important lessons that we perhaps didn't achieve in our previous lifetimes."

Gloria paused. "Some lifetimes you will be born male, other times you will be female. Sometimes you will be born into privileged homes, other times you will be born into hardship.

Each circumstance offers your soul different opportunities to learn and grow."

My mind was reeling with this entirely new perspective that Gloria was presenting to me.

"So, the people that are in my family, have they always been with me or do they change each time?"

"We frequently belong to the same 'soul group' as certain people in our lives. You will often, although not always, incarnate together into the same lifetime, but you may play different roles each time. For example, your son or daughter may have been your father or mother in previous lifetimes."

Gloria continued. "The parents we're born to are no coincidence. Our parents, and the circumstances we're born into each lifetime, enable us to learn something important about ourselves, and subsequently give us the opportunity to grow spiritually."

I sat there with my mind racing over what Gloria was saying. I was thinking about my choice to become a professional homeopath and wondered if this was relevant to helping my children in this lifetime.

"So, were my children born to me so I can help them?" I asked.

Gloria smiled and replied with amusement, "On the contrary, they have come to help you!"

I felt foolish and arrogant. I had automatically assumed that being the adult and their mother, my role was to help my children, but this was only a part of the story.

"Sometimes, although not always, our children are more evolved and wiser than we are. Either way, both parent and child are together to learn important lessons from each other during this lifetime."

It was partway through my many questions, and Gloria's comprehensive answers, that she began to look increasingly agitated. She explained that spirit people were there to answer my questions, but she was becoming frustrated with them. She leaned forward placing her tea mug back on the table, then slid forwards in her seat suddenly. She ducked her head lower, and flapped her hand back and forth near her ear. She appeared irritated as she said "stop it, stop it" with a stern look on her face. Apparently, the spirit people were talking too loudly in her ear, and the answers were coming too rapidly, and in great detail. I was baffled, if not slightly alarmed at her frustration, the change in her mood, and the speed at which she began talking. She stood up and began pacing up and down the room in front of the sofa where she had been sitting. She said walking helped her when she was relaying messages like this. It was a surreal few minutes. Watching her I began to silently question her sanity, and yet I was equally fascinated by the level of knowledge and eloquence in the answers that she was giving me.

At some point during our conversations, the subject turned to homeopathy. She started to talk about homeopathic practices and philosophies in such detail, she couldn't possibly have known that level of information without studying the subject in the same depth I had. In fact, she wasn't even 'talking' about it, this homeopathic information was rapidly pouring out of her mouth. She admitted that she knew nothing about homeopathy herself, but the spirit people who were communicating were very experienced in the subject. She explained the knowledge and answers were coming *through* her, not *from* her. She was the 'medium', the 'conduit' between this world, and the spirit world. The spirit *world*? She'd mentioned that earlier. What was that? I was puzzled, and concerned. I began to wonder if meeting her in my home was a bad idea. If these spirit people were talking to her now, that meant they were in my house! I had heard stories over the years about never using an Ouija board in your own home as it could bring in unwanted spirits. Wasn't this similar? Could these spirits now come and go because I'd allowed this psychic lady into my home? My fears were running rampant through my mind.

Once Gloria had finished passing messages from spirit people, she settled down again on the sofa. The conversation returned to a normal pace.

I asked her, "What's it like to live as a psychic medium, seeing and hearing things that others can't?"

"Actually, my psychic abilities only started about five years ago. I haven't told my family as they wouldn't approve. I don't mention it to work colleagues either. The only people who know me as a psychic are those who attend the spiritualist church services I lead, or the spiritualist college I lecture at, or those who join my psychic development workshops."

"So, how did it first start? How did you know you were psychic?" I was curious to know more about her experiences.

"Honestly, I thought I was going mad," she said. "I could hear voices in my head. It took a while for me to realize what was happening. I then trained at the spiritualist college as I felt it was important to have the credibility of being a certified psychic medium."

I wasn't immune to how crazy these comments made her sound, but I continued.

"How do you manage the voices in your head now? How do you manage your privacy? Can you switch it on and off?" I was genuinely curious to understand more about her experiences.

"Not really. They still wake me up in the night."

I didn't like the sound of this at all. Surely not all psychic people were being woken up by spirit people every night. This just didn't seem right to me.

"It's amazing, but it must be quite a responsibility having this gift?"

"Absolutely. Personal responsibility is, in my opinion, one of the most important spiritual principles," she said. "Just recently a man visited me for a psychic reading. He was talking about his son's upcoming wedding, and I could see that his father was going to pass unexpectedly very soon. It was not my place to tell him about his father's death, so I used this knowledge to remind him to treasure all of his relationships."

I was taken aback by the thought that she could foresee people's death. "Do you know the date of your own death?" I asked.

"Yes, and that's like a death sentence, let me tell you. I would have preferred not to know, but I asked spirit and they told me."

It was during this conversation that Gloria dropped a bombshell that was to change my life forever. "Your daughter is a psychic-medium too," she told me. Faith was only four years old at this time. "In fact," she added, "your son is too, but he's not as tuned into spirit as your daughter. Tom was only two years old. I stared at her blankly, unsure what to think, let alone comment. This was a bizarre and awkward conversation, and not for the first time during our meeting, I began to wish I hadn't invited her to my home.

She continued, "Many children are born with psychic abilities, but these can fade or disappear completely as they grow older. Often the adults around them don't believe what their children are telling them. They assume it's just a child's imagination or invisible friends."

My mind was spinning. I spent all day, nearly every day with my children and there was no reason to suspect they had any special 'psychic' abilities. Neither of them appeared to talk to imaginary friends and neither appeared 'different' to other children. The only quality that stood out as being different to her friends was that Faith seemed very gentle and mature for her age. An 'old soul' as someone called her when she was a baby.

My thoughts momentarily turned to my husband, Paul. He was never going to believe this conversation. He knew I had invited Gloria to the house to talk about the book, but he far from believed anything about past lives or psychic matters. He often joked about the fact his once 'normal' wife had become a bit more 'hippy' since becoming a homeopath some years before.

Paul had been totally supportive of me training and practicing as a homeopath and also (albeit with an amused twinkle in his eye) when I told him I was going to join other students on my homeopathy course who were beginning their reiki healer training with Karen, the spiritual friend I had met. Telling him he may have psychic children would be a step too far, although potentially highly entertaining!

Fortunately, Gloria didn't venture into detail about my children's abilities, but she did encourage me to ask Faith about it. It seemed odd to me. Surely I would know if Faith was psychic? Surely Faith would have said something over the past four years, which I could have used to connect the dots, to make sense of Gloria's comments. If she was seeing or hearing people, why hadn't she asked me about them?

The morning had flown by and it was time for me to collect the children from nursery school, so I thanked Gloria for coming, and was relieved when her visit was over. I felt like I'd just spent the past few hours in a strange dream, and I was keen to wake up and forget all about it!

The idea of my children seeing or hearing a spirit world that I had never heard of seemed ridiculous. Once again, I felt myself questioning Gloria's state of mind, and yet I had a nagging feeling within me that wouldn't let me completely dismiss her comments as nonsense.

When I told my mother what Gloria had said about Faith, she was pleasantly surprised! Having visited a few psychic-mediums over the years, she was very open-minded to their abilities and the idea of life after death, but her knowledge was limited to her own experiences with them. On the contrary, my husband Paul was very quiet when I relayed to him what Gloria and I had discussed that day. Psychic matters were definitely out of his comfort zone, but he listened politely. He was, as expected, completely skeptical about a spirit world existing, never mind his children having any psychic abilities, but he was happy for me to approach the subject with Faith as that was, of course, the quickest way to settle the matter and move on.

In the week that followed, I mulled over all the different things Gloria had told me during her visit. I intended to ask Faith, but I was avoiding it. I didn't know how to broach the subject and, if I was honest, I wasn't sure I wanted to. How would I ask a four-year-old a question like that? And what if I didn't like the answer? I still got goose bumps thinking of the creepy ghost stories my friends and cousins shared with me growing up. The idea of discussing invisible spirit people with a young child was surely going to scare her as much as it did me. Despite my best efforts to ignore what Gloria had told me, her comments continued to circulate in my mind. I knew that I needed to raise the subject with Faith so I could put the matter to rest, but it was several weeks after meeting Gloria, before I finally conceded.

ASKING FAITH

The evening I chose to raise the subject with Faith, she was playing quietly on the floor in her bedroom. She loved playing with small plastic figures, and spent hours creating families and acting out role-plays. I felt awkward as I entered her bedroom and sat on her bed. I watched her playing for a few moments, until she stopped and looked up at me. My heart was pounding but I tried to look relaxed and calm. It wasn't going to help the situation if I appeared terrified before we'd started the conversation!

I told her casually about the lady who had come to visit, and what she had told me. Faith listened quietly as I talked, occasionally she looked up at me, but otherwise she continued looking down at the figures in her hands. Despite my attempts to keep the conversation as natural as possible, she could sense my unease and the seriousness to my questions.

"Is it true? Can you see people in the room with us now?" I asked, trying to keep my voice calm. The idea of people standing next to me whom I couldn't see was alarming, and my mind was racing back to the many horror movies I'd watched in my teens and that reinforced my fear of anything otherworldly.

Faith didn't look up from her figures. She nodded her head and said, "Yes."

"You didn't even look."

She glanced up at me and said matter-of-factly, "I don't need to look to see them. I know when they're there." Then she looked straight back at her figures again and continued her play.

"Can you hear them?"

"Yes." She continued playing with her figures.

"Whom do you see?" I asked.

"Lots of people," she said.

I thought about my granddad who had died a few years earlier, of whom Faith was fond. "Do you ever see Great-granddad?"

"Yes, all the time."

"Really? Does he talk to you?" The idea of my granddad talking to Faith was much more comforting to me than strange unknown spirits.

She stopped playing and looked up at me. "He reads me stories at night-time, and we play games together."

"Why didn't you tell me you could see him?" Surely she would have mentioned this to me if she really could see people who had died?

Faith shrugged. She couldn't understand my interest. She seemed bored by our conversation and more interested in the figures she was playing with.

"Does he look the same?"

"Yes, but his hair is much darker."

This was a surreal conversation to be having with my daughter, bordering on the ridiculous. Yet, despite the skeptical side of my mind trying to discredit what she was saying, questioning if I was just creating the situation by the way I was asking her, I could see she wasn't spinning me a story. She wasn't embellishing her answers, she wasn't reveling in my attention, she wasn't even that forthcoming with information. She was giving me simple, short, matter-of-fact answers, which were of little interest to her. It was as if I was asking her what games she played at school today. She didn't seem interested in talking about it, and just wanted to continue playing with her figures. She had no idea that her answers were rocking my world.

Before I left her room, I explained to Faith that although there were other children and adults who could see and hear spirit people too, her friends and family could not see those things. Hearing these words, she looked at me surprised. She hadn't realized she was different.

As I left her room, I paused outside her bedroom door and took a long, deep breath. I felt as if I was back in that bizarre dream again and desperately wanted to wake up, but this time, I couldn't. A can of worms had just been irreversibly opened, perhaps only a little, but opened all the same. What now?

Waves of nausea washed over me. Disturbed by these recent conversations, I felt deeply anxious, as in the past when receiving sad or upsetting news. It couldn't be happening. I wanted to drop the whole subject and go back to my family life the way it had been before I met Gloria. This was absurd, I thought. What was I getting involved with here?

When I told Paul he listened politely to everything that I discovered, but he remained skeptical and unconvinced that it was true. He thought that Faith must be simply playing along with my suggestions and telling me what I wanted to hear. He wasn't sure what to think, but he was naturally inclined to step back from such 'suspicious nonsense' and whilst he continued to listen patiently to my updates, he didn't talk to Faith about it directly. When I raised this with him, he said this was partly because Faith was usually asleep or settled in bed ready to turn lights out when he came home from work and partly he feared the answer he might get. He expected Faith to either admit she was playing a game with Mummy and had been making it all up, in which case he'd have to break the news to me, or worst still, she might tell him, "There's somebody standing behind you, Daddy," which he was terrified of hearing!

For the next few weeks I practically slept with one eye open! The conversation with Faith had unsettled me and I was struggling to sleep at night. All I could think about were spirit people potentially being around me and I scared myself so much I was becoming a nervous wreck! On the other hand, I kept reminding myself that my young children apparently settled to sleep quite happily despite *seeing* these spirit people in our home! They weren't scared at bedtimes, they didn't beg me to stay in their rooms, both of which I would expect if they were frightened. I was caught between wanting to protect my children, and wanting to run a mile from the situation! What should I do about spirit people in their bedrooms? Were they safe? How should I manage this? I wasn't sure what my children were experiencing exactly, but I wanted to understand more. If Faith's psychic abilities were real, then we needed to know how to talk to her about it, and how to help her if required. I needed to learn as much as I could about psychic abilities and the spirit world. As Gloria was the only psychic I knew, it made sense for me to ask for her advice.

THE LITTLE GIRL

Some weeks later, Gloria joined my children and me on a walk around woodland managed by the Forestry Commission near where we live. Gloria had agreed to answer more of my questions, to help me learn more about Faith's abilities and the spirit world in general.

As we were walking through the woods, Gloria told me that she had asked the spirit people about Faith's psychic abilities, and had been told, "She lives as much in this world as she does in the spirit world." She explained that Faith didn't yet realize the worlds were different. She was able to see, hear and sense spirit. She had full interaction as if they were in the room like living people. Gloria also mentioned again that my son Tom could also see spirit, but he wasn't sure what he was seeing as he was just two years old.

I found these conversations about the spirit world fascinating, overwhelming and rather frightening. I did my best to hide my fears, but the thought of spirit people existing and being around us rattled me. Who was interacting with my daughter? Who were these spirits? Were they good or bad, male or female? I had no idea about this part of her life at all, I felt helpless to either help her, or protect her if needed. I felt like I had entered some alternate reality where my life was not what it seemed.

Gloria laughed when I told her this. "Yes, it's like *The Matrix*," she said, referring to the movie where Keanu Reeves's character must decide if he wants to live in the world he has always known, or the 'real' world that he was previously unaware existed. At this point, I very much wanted to continue living in my 'normal' world, and pretend that a 'spirit world' didn't exist at all.

After our walk, we stopped for a picnic on a busy grassed area with lots of families and children. My children ran into the little patch of trees just next to the picnic area. They were playing quite happily, and I could watch them from where we sat. Gloria told me there was a little girl trying to play with Faith, but she was ignoring her and the little girl was getting upset about it. This seemed odd because Faith was a shy, gentle child and hurting another child's feelings would seem out of character, but Gloria explained it was a 'spirit' child trying to play with Faith.

Not quite sure what to make of this, and not wanting to put Faith on the spot with an audience, I waited until Gloria had left, then I approached Faith in the trees to ask her quietly about it.

"Faith, is there a little spirit girl trying to play with you?" Faith stopped and stared at me in surprise. She nodded to confirm this was the case. What a bizarre situation. I thought now what? Has she said that just because I asked, or is there really a little spirit girl there? I tried to maintain a 'normal' conversation for all our sakes and suggested Faith might let her join in. Faith nodded again. I gave the children a few more minutes to play whilst I walked back to the picnic area trying to gather my thoughts.

Was I perpetuating the crazy idea of Faith seeing spirits or was it really happening? Was Faith only answering my questions about her psychic abilities because it was what she thought I wanted to hear, or was it real? If she could really see spirit people, why didn't she volunteer information throughout the day, why was information only forthcoming when I questioned her?

Nothing seemed normal anymore. I felt helpless and out of my depth, and longed for the way my life was before I'd met Gloria, and I was concerned about the impact my questions were having on Faith.

As has now become routine in our family, when I'm tucking Faith into bed is when she's calm and open to conversations about spirit. That night, at bedtime, I asked her gently about the little girl.

"How long have you known this little girl?"

Faith was sitting up in bed, ready for her story. "I don't know. She's always been with me," she replied.

"How old is she?"

She shrugged and turned to look at me. "She's five, like me. She goes to school with me, and plays at home with me, too." Faith had only recently started school. "Well that's really nice that you have a friend to help you settle at school," I said. "What does she look like?"

"She has long dark hair in pigtails, and she always wears the same dress with little flowers."

I nodded as I pictured the girl in my mind. "What's the little girl's name?"

"I don't know her name."

"Really? You play with her all the time, but you don't know her name?" Whilst I knew Faith's shy nature meant she was unlikely to ask another child their name directly, I was surprised she hadn't learned of this girl's name, given she apparently played with her so much.

"I just think of her and she comes to me."

I felt sad at the thought a little girl was in the spirit world and visiting Faith all by herself, when she too was so young. "Do you know why she is in the spirit world?" Since our initial conversation, I had gradually begun talking a little about the spirit world with Faith.

Faith turned to look at the side of her bed opposite to where I was kneeling beside her. After a moment she looked back at me and said calmly, "She says she died in a fire."

I was shocked. For a few moments I froze whilst this statement sank in. Firstly, I hadn't realized the little girl was in the room with us. That alone had my nerves jangling, but also this was the first time Faith had relayed a 'real time' conversation from a spirit to me. Until now, I only knew they visited or played with her throughout her day. I was also shocked because Faith had only recently turned five years old and we had never talked about the ways in which people could die, not to mention children dying. My mind was spinning as I contemplated where else she might have heard the subject, but I knew in my heart that it wasn't her imagination. It was something about the way she was relaying the information. It was factual, not embellished with a five-year-old's imagination. The idea of a child dying in a fire was a world apart from Faith's usual conversations. It was at this point I began to truly accept the possibility that my daughter could see and communicate with people I couldn't.

Faith was very calm, but I stopped asking questions at that point. I was too frightened to cause any detail to be revealed that might upset her, and too frightened to know any more myself! I was not sure what I expected, but the idea that a little girl who had died could be standing right next to us as we were talking about her, was very strange.

I was keen to keep the conversation with Faith as natural as possible, so I finished with, "Well, how lovely that this little girl is your friend and goes to school with you, too." I kissed her goodnight and left the room.

Outside her door, I hesitated. Again I had a strange feeling knowing I was potentially leaving my daughter in a room with spirits who were strangers to me, but that this was also 'normal' for Faith. She was a shy girl around living people, but seemed to feel perfectly safe with the spirits. As much as it was bizarre and a little frightening for me, there was a chink of light filtering in where my mind had previously been closed. I thought if it was all indeed true, perhaps I should feel comforted that Faith was happy with, and maybe even looked after by, those friends I couldn't see.

Now, some years later, we know that this little girl's name is Jane, and she is Faith's main spirit guide who helps keep her safe and accompanies Faith on her life journey. Jane is always the same age as Faith, and she is always wearing the same dress with pink and green flowers. We also now know that Jane and her younger brother were both killed in a fire at their grandmother's house. Somebody left the stove on and it caught fire overnight. Their parents, who were not in the house at the time, survived them and have only recently passed into spirit. Faith has told me they have been reunited with their children.

THE NURSE

In the weeks that followed, despite having talked to Faith about the people she could see, life continued largely as normal. I had hoped that maybe she would begin telling us about the spirit people that visited us, but she didn't volunteer any information about them at all. Only when I asked her would she talk about them, and only then to answer my questions, which she did both calmly and without much interest. She clearly didn't understand my curiosity, seeing spirits wasn't strange to her.

One evening I was driving Faith and Tom home from a children's party. We had reached a neighboring village and I was suddenly struck by the strongest smell of antiseptic cream. It filled my nostrils and in fact the whole car. I opened the car windows to see if perhaps the smell was outside, but it wasn't. As soon as I closed the windows it was very strong again.

I was puzzled about where this smell was coming from because we didn't use medical antiseptic creams, only natural homeopathic ones. It wasn't a big deal, but the smell was so strong, it just seemed really strange. I had stayed at the party and wasn't aware of any incident with antiseptic that might explain the smell.

"Did anybody put any cream on you at the party?" I asked the children, glancing at them in my rear-view mirror

They both looked at me blankly. "No," they both chimed.

I was still puzzled. The smell wasn't wearing off. It was still as strong as ever.

Then I had a thought. "Faith, is there somebody in the car with us?" She didn't answer me, so I glanced back at her. She was looking shy and embarrassed and just nodded awkwardly.

"Can you tell me who it is?"

She didn't look keen to talk, but she reluctantly answered, "It's coming from the nurse."

After a series of questions, Faith confirmed there was a nurse sitting in the front passenger seat next to me! She told me she had short curly dark hair and wore a white hat. She was wearing a nurse uniform, with a green cross. I didn't understand the green cross, as I'd only ever known nurses with a red cross, but Faith was quite sure the cross was green, not red.

I didn't know why the nurse was visiting, but I could smell her so clearly. She stayed with us for about twenty minutes. The antiseptic smell disappeared as suddenly as it had arrived.

The nurse visited me several times over the next few months. On one of these occasions when Faith was with me, I took the opportunity to ask who she was. Faith turned to look across the room and paused as she listened.

"She says her name is Madeleine, but you always called her 'Maddy'…you were good friends…she says you were both nurses in the war…you worked together near the front line."

I sat in amazement. I had never heard about my own past-life experiences before. Faith was only five or six years old at this time, long before she knew anything about war or 'the front line'.

To this day, the nurse still visits me. Whenever I smell antiseptic cream with no other explanation, I know that Maddy has popped by. I have asked Faith if Maddy wants to tell me anything, but she always tells me, "No, she just wanted to see you."

As it happens, despite my lack of experience with anything psychic, that wasn't the first time I had been aware of a distinctive scent belonging to someone who had died.

Before Faith was born, although I had no prior knowledge of anything spiritual, I did have a spiritual experience that I couldn't explain away. Three months before my wedding my maternal grandmother passed away suddenly from a stroke. It was completely unexpected and I felt her loss deeply. We had been very close in my childhood years, spending time together most days. I was particularly sad as she would have loved to have been at my wedding and now she would be unable to be there.

One evening, shortly after our wedding, I was sitting watching TV with Paul. During the advert break, I went upstairs to fetch something from our bedroom and the strongest scent of my nan hit me. It was overwhelming, and completely unmistakable. My nan was a heavy smoker, so I thought maybe somebody was smoking outside in the road, but when I checked the bedroom windows they were all shut tight and there was no smell of cigarette smoke outside at all. In the room, however, the smell was very strong. It wasn't just cigarette smell either, it was the scent of Nan.

Feeling emotional, I called out to Paul asking him to come upstairs. As he walked into the room he too could smell cigarette smoke clearly. Wondering what all the excitement was, our dog then ran upstairs and, as he came through the door, his ears went back and he whined and ran downstairs frightened. That's when I realized it was really my nan. Tears rolled down my face. I sat on the corner of the bed and felt the most incredible calm feeling come over me. I remember sitting there and describing to Paul how I could feel my nan stroking my hair and down my back. It was a lovely feeling and incredibly comforting. It lasted for perhaps five minutes, and then she was gone again.

Since that time, my mother and I have frequently experienced this scent of my grandmother combined with the smell of cigarettes. Nobody in my family smokes, so it's quite easy to know when she has come to see us. In recent years, Faith has told me many times how she often sees Nan at my mother's house.

Interestingly, in my teenage years, many years before my grandmother had passed, I also recall her telling me about a similar experience of her own. Some months after my grandfather had died, my nan returned home after walking their Jack Russell terrier. Granddad had always been the dog walker, but when he died, Nan reluctantly took over the dog-walking duties. On this occasion, as she returned home, she opened the back door to a strong odor of Granddad's shampoo. She knew she wasn't imagining it, because the dog became very excited, barking and running around their house, frantically searching for Granddad, but of course he wasn't there. At least not physically.

In recent years, I had a similar experience with my maternal grandfather. He was a quiet, stubborn man who 'called a spade a spade' as my father would say, but with plenty of patience for my siblings and me when we stayed over. When he needed some peace and quiet he retreated to his garage to work on restoring the classic motorcycles he loved so much. About nine years after my nan passed, and twenty-two years after my granddad passed, I walked upstairs one evening and into the bathroom within my home and the strongest scent hit me as I entered. I remember spinning around the room smelling the air, ecstatic because I recognized the smell as belonging to Granddad whom I hadn't seen or heard from since I was fifteen years old. My memories of him came flooding back instantly. I can't explain what smell it was, but it was quite unmistakable. A mixture of his Brylcreem and cigarettes, a smell that was totally unique to him! It was wonderful. I don't know why it took him so long to make contact with me, but I was delighted that he had come to visit.

As my knowledge of the spirit world has grown, these experiences have taught me that even when our loved ones have passed into spirit, they are often nearby and continue to visit us regularly. They are never 'gone' as we sometimes believe. My nan wouldn't have missed my wedding for anything in the world. I know now that she was right there by my side during my special day, even though I didn't know it at the time.

SPIRITUAL CHURCH

In the months that followed that first meeting with Gloria, with the aim of understanding my daughter's gift and the spirit world she was interacting with, I started learning as much as I could about it. Gloria loaned me books, which I devoured with great interest, eager to learn more and genuinely fascinated by what I was reading. I started scouring the bookshelves in town, and began to develop an interest in other books with a 'spiritual' link, including more Brian Weiss books which he wrote following the success of *Many Lives, Many Masters*.

I visited local spiritualist churches who regularly ran an 'open circle night'. Open circle is the name given to occasions when people who are interested in learning more about the spirit world can meet to practice psychic-mediumship skills. An 'open' circle usually means anybody interested can attend, usually for a very small donation towards the church. For those more experienced with mediumship, there are 'closed circles' which are by invitation only. The participants of closed circles are usually mediums with advanced skills, and they work together to improve their skills of communicating with the spirit world.

Local spiritual churches also offer mediumship evenings where anybody can attend to watch an experienced medium in action. They usually stand on a stage, if the church has one, and the audience watches and listens as messages from the spirit world are communicated via the medium to people in the room. These local churches also offer 'open platform' nights where budding mediums can practice their skills in front of a sympathetic audience.

It was at one of these spiritual churches that I attended a workshop for beginners. I was filled with anticipation. I had no idea what to expect. The church was unlike any church I had visited before. It was very small and relatively modern compared to the old stone village churches that I was familiar with as a child. As I stepped inside it took a few moments for my eyes to adjust to the darkness, a contrast to the bright sunshine outside. The building was mainly one long narrow room, with a kitchen and a smaller room at the far end. The main room was mostly empty with just a few ladies and several men dotted around the rows of chairs, all of whom were waiting for the workshop to begin. A well-known local medium called Linda, who I had been told was well respected, was running the workshop.

Linda introduced herself and gathered us all at the front of the church nearest the stage. She was not what I expected at all. *She looks so normal!* I thought. A young, attractive lady with long dark hair and blue eyes, she was welcoming and friendly. In passing, she mentioned that she had two young children and I liked her immediately. I felt I could relate to her, like someone I would chat to comfortably outside the school gates.

Linda explained how we would all have an opportunity to stand on the stage and work with spirit. *This could be interesting*, I thought. I had absolutely no idea how I was going to do that. When Linda asked who would like to go first, mine was the only hand that popped up. I had no idea what I was doing, but was eager to learn. I was there to find out as much as I could about spirit, so I could understand Faith's experiences better, and was willing to throw myself into the deep end, to learn fast.

As I climbed the four or five steps onto the stage, I could feel adrenalin charging through my body, and my legs trembled with nerves. I stood looking out at the small audience of workshop participants sitting in the front rows of seats. Linda explained that she would be helping me. She stood diagonally a meter behind me on the stage, holding her palms out towards me. Out of nowhere, the strangest sensation overcame me. My whole body felt like somebody had just plugged me into the electric and I was suddenly buzzing and filled with energy. As a Reiki healer, I was familiar with the gentle warm feeling of energy being sent from one individual to another, but this 'buzzing' was on a higher level, much, much stronger and quite forceful. The feeling running through my body was so unusual that I hastily described it to my fellow participants.

Linda then said, "There is somebody here from spirit, can you tell the others what you feel?"

At that moment, I could picture a lady. It felt much the same as when you remember someone you know, who isn't with you at that moment, except I didn't know who the lady was as she was just an image in my mind.

Linda encouraged me to describe what I was seeing so I told her about the image.

"Well done, yes, it is a lady," Linda confirmed.

As I stood there, I felt my body changing, rather like the character Violet in *Charlie and Chocolate Factory* when she blows up like a balloon.

"Something is happening to me," I said with astonishment and a measure of concern. I turned and looked at Linda for reassurance.

"Just tell us what you feel," she said.

"I feel much bigger, like I'm growing outwards," I replied. "My cheeks are changing too, it's so strange. I want to scrunch up my cheeks into little tight balls." Outwardly, to those watching me, I wouldn't look any different, I was only inwardly changing shape. It was the most bizarre and disconcerting sensation.

I continued to describe the image I could see. "The lady has the same high cheeks as the sensation I'm personally experiencing – little rosy-red pert cheeks. She has a smiling face and is a happy lady. She's bigger than me, plump with smiley eyes."

I was astounded at how clearly I could see the lady pictured in my mind, and I was desperately trying to find the words to describe her so others in the room could understand what I was seeing and someone could recognize who she was. I was conscious that if I was too vague with my details, or if

I misjudged something about her, it might have hindered someone in the audience recognizing their deceased loved one, and subsequently weaken the credibility of the message the spirit person wanted to communicate.

More details came to me. "I see her wearing a floral dress, it comes down to her calves, and the dress is covered with pink flowers. She's walking down the road with a walking stick that has patterns on it, possibly flowers, too. Her hair is grey, thick, curly, and short, and those rosy cheeks... My own cheeks feel so strange!"

"Very good," said Linda. "Can you tell the audience who she is? She belongs to somebody here. Can you feel who she was to them?"

I had no idea what she meant. How could I possibly know who this spirit lady was to someone?

After a while Linda said, "That feeling is the 'mother' feeling. Remember that 'mother' feeling for next time, as you will begin to recognize it."

"Okay," I said, but I still wasn't sure I recognized what she was talking about.

"Can you feel who she is here to visit? Who does she want to talk to?" Linda prompted me again.

I looked around the room, but I didn't know how to choose anybody.

After a few moments Linda asked, "Does anybody in the audience recognize the description?"

A lady put her hand up, and it was only then I recognized the family likeness to the image in my mind. She too had a smiley face and small rosy cheeks, but was much younger with different hair.

"She looks a bit like you!" I gushed with disbelief. "How amazing!" The lady in the audience nodded, smiling at me.

Linda kept me on track. "You've provided the evidence of who this lady is, now can you give her the message her mother has for her?" Many spiritualist churches are members of the SNU (Spiritualists National Union) and one of the principles they follow is to provide evidence of the existence of life after death, so Linda was making sure we were following the correct SNU protocol.

In my mind, the image changed. It was as if I was standing outside in the dark, looking in through a small window of a home, watching a lady work. The lady I could see wasn't the 'mother' anymore, it was her daughter, the lady in the audience. In my mind, I could see her sitting inside a warm cozy room. It was evening and the room was dimly lit, as if by candlelight. I wasn't sure exactly what she was doing, but it looked like she was either writing a letter, or doing needlework. Whatever it was, she was concentrating deeply and focusing on her work.

I had absolutely no idea what the message was. I described what I could see, but it didn't make any sense to me.

Linda took over at that point. As an experienced psychic-medium, she understood the message. She looked towards the lady in the audience. "Your mother is telling you that she wants you to take better care of your eyes. You're damaging your eyes because you're working in the dark, and you need more light when you're working."

'Seriously?' I thought. I was surprised the message could be so trivial, so I was skeptical about the accuracy, but the lady in the audience was very happy with it.

"Do you understand this message?" Linda asked her.

The lady nodded, smiling. "Yes, thank you very much." She knew exactly what we were talking about, and thanked us for bringing her mother through.

As fast as the electric had switched on, it switched off again. Now we had finished working with this spirit lady, Linda was no longer holding her palms towards me, and I could no longer feel the 'buzzing' energy through my body. I walked back down the steps and joined the group again who were sitting in front of the stage. It was somebody else's turn.

I was astonished. How had I just done that? It must have been the energy the medium gave to me. What a bizarre, but exhilarating experience, not only to have seen a spirit lady in my mind so clearly, but to 'feel' what she looked like – my body growing bigger, and my cheeks getting higher.

PAUL

I went home from the spiritual workshop that night gushing to Paul about my experiences, and those of my fellow participants. We all had slightly different experiences, and by watching each other that day, we had learned so much more about how communications with the spirit world worked.

As always, Paul listened patiently and politely to everything I had to say, and he was pleased that I'd enjoyed my day, but he really didn't know what to think. After reading so many books on the subjects, and now this experience at the spiritual church, I was clearly moving both feet into the 'I believe in spirit world' camp, whereas he still had both feet in the 'there must be another explanation' camp. He didn't know what he believed. He'd never given it much thought, and he still wasn't comfortable thinking about it. He was raised within a family skeptical of psychic matters, and with no experiences of his own to draw on, he was less inclined to accept my experiences as evidence that psychics and the after life were real. If it hadn't been scientifically proven, and widely accepted by most grounded people (not my hippy 'alternative' type), then he was doubtful there could be such a thing as a spirit world, and there must surely be another logical explanation for my experiences.

My strengthening belief that the spirit world was indeed real was founded on my own experiences, together with my conversations with Faith about the spirit people who visited her. Paul hadn't partaken in either of these, and although he respected my views, they were different to his own. He found it easier to surmise that perhaps Faith just had a wild imagination, and all of us who attended the spiritual workshop had been unwittingly duped; that we went to the spiritual church far too open-minded and willing to be led down the garden path. For now, Paul was keeping his feet firmly planted where they had always been, on the ground.

Despite the close relationship Paul shares with Faith and Tom, neither of them have ever voluntarily discussed the subject of the spirit world directly with him. Some years ago, Paul attempted to discuss the subject with Faith one bedtime, mainly to reassure her that it was okay to talk to him about it, but she clammed up. She listened to what he had to say, but she didn't offer him any evidence of her abilities at all.

Another time, he joined Faith and me at bedtime and listened to the questions that we were asking spirit, and the answers that Faith received from them. Despite a significant amount of information being provided at speed through Faith, without time for her imagination to be involved and most of which was not typical of Faith's vocabulary, Paul was still waiting for the concrete evidence he needed before he was ready to definitively agree that spirit people existed and lived alongside us.

Although it would be lovely to hear him agree that the spirit world is indeed real, I also recognize that Paul and his skepticism bring an important quality to our family. Put simply, he is our rock. He is a gentle, calm, stable, balanced, grounding energy that the children and I need to keep our feet on the ground.

Whilst we communicate with spirit people, it's also very important that we continue living our lives the same way as others around us, at school, at work, and in our community. I believe it's very important to stay grounded. We were after all born into this world to live this life, with all of its lessons. If we spend too much time focusing on the spirit world, we may miss valuable opportunities to grow and develop here in the physical world.

More information on 'grounding' can be found in the chapter, 'Sensitive to Our Environment – Protecting Our Energy'.

Although Paul has a different point of view to mine, he is always respectful when I talk to him about the children's interactions with the spirit world, and quietly supportive of me exploring this journey with them. We are both very aware of the influence our conversations about spirit world can have on their wider lives, and he trusts me to manage that carefully. Many times, when I have been unsure how to handle a situation with the children, he offers a balanced viewpoint, so together we can help make the right decisions for the children.

Our lives truly are a combination of the perfectly 'ordinary' with occasional 'extraordinary' moments dropped in.

SHARING OUR SECRET

Raising two young children with the ability to communicate with spirit is not without its challenges. Whilst the children and I are very comfortable and proud of their mediumship abilities, it can be difficult confiding in others, as not everybody feels the same way.

Understandably, for a society which doesn't really talk about life after death, on the few occasions I have confided in friends or family about the children's psychic abilities, I was met with raised eyebrows, confused, nervous glances, and skepticism. "Oh, I don't believe in any of that nonsense," one friend said to me sharply and cut the conversation. Other people were politely skeptical, but they swiftly changed the subject without asking any questions. It was like having the door slammed in my face before I could even discuss it with them. Their reactions left me feeling embarrassed and isolated.

Although some of my friends from Homeopathy college were more 'open-minded' when I mentioned our psychic experiences to them, they knew nothing about the subject which could be helpful to me. My friend Karen who had first introduced me to spiritual matters at college gasped when I mentioned it to her. "I see dead people!" she said in mock horror, quoting from the movie *The Sixth Sense,* which involves a young child tormented by terrifying spirits. So, I soon discovered that it was much easier not to mention this side of our lives to others.

Although Paul was supportive of me exploring spiritual matters, he didn't have an interest in learning about it himself, though he was willing to listen to me talk about it. My parents were both interested in what I told them, but didn't know how to help.

Unlike my passion for learning more about the subject, and my desire to share our experiences, Faith has always been very private about her psychic abilities. In her twelve years, I have only known her mention her gift to a friend once. We had a neighbor's son Jonny around for dinner one evening when Faith was about five years old. They were sitting at the table in the garden eating dinner, and from the kitchen I could hear Faith getting upset. When I hurried outside, she told me that Jonny didn't believe that her great-granddad was sitting in the chair next to him. Jonny, understandably was perfectly confident she was wrong as he couldn't see anyone sitting there. Faith, meanwhile was distraught that he didn't believe her.

It was an important lesson for all of us, especially Faith. That day she learnt first-hand how friends can react when they can't see or hear what she does. Since that day, she has never told anyone of her psychic abilities and she will only discuss it with her close family. I have no doubt that one day Faith will use her gift to help others, in a way with which she is comfortable. For now, Faith is happy for her experiences to be shared in this book, in the hope it helps people understand that their loved ones continue to be part of their lives after death, and to bring comfort and share knowledge of our experiences with other families of psychic children.

Unlike Faith's reserved nature, Tom has inherited my openness, and being several years younger than Faith, he took longer to learn the implications of sharing our psychic abilities with others. One time, the teachers at the infant school he attended were creating a book to sell to parents and they had asked each child to write down what made them special, so this could be included in it. One of my friends was head of the parents and teacher's fundraising committee that was collating the responses from the children. I had previously confided in her about Faith's abilities, but she was very skeptical and so we hadn't discussed it again. She called me one afternoon to explain that Tom had written, "I am special because I see spirits" and asked me if I really wanted her to print that in a book for all parents to see. The tone of her voice spoke volumes. Whilst I was hugely appreciative that she gave me the opportunity to decide if I wanted Tom's entry to be printed in the book, I felt the weight of her judgment on me as a parent. I didn't want to be responsible for putting my child in a situation which could potentially cause him ridicule at school, and I was embarrassed that my skeptical disapproving friend had 'caught' the book entry before printing, and stopped our family secret becoming inadvertently known by everyone in the village.

Another time, when Tom was five years old, Paul and I were visiting the teacher for parents' evening to discuss Tom's progress and see his work. Shortly after we sat down with his teacher, she explained to us rather awkwardly how part way through a math's exercise Tom had turned to his teacher and explained his great-granddad had just arrived in the room. When she questioned him about it, he admitted he could see spirit people sometimes and his great-granddad was standing right there. She had no idea what to make of it.

I was speechless for a few moments as she caught me off-guard and I was not expecting to discuss this at parents' evening. Paul sat next to me quiet as a mouse, leaving me to answer! I stumbled through my words, honestly but awkwardly. "Oh, yes…we have unusual abilities in our family…the children both see spirits…always have…it's just we don't normally share that with others, so I wasn't expecting Tom to mention it." I think the teacher was expecting a more logical explanation, so she was quite shocked as she listened to me, and then she stumbled through her own answer. "Oh, I see, well…we're all different." She smiled awkwardly.

As a parent, it has been difficult at times to know whether hiding the truth about the children's abilities from the friends, neighbors and teachers around us is the right thing to do, or not. Honesty is such an important quality for me to instill in my children, yet I deliberately choose not to mention the spiritual side of our lives to most of the people we spend time with. My expectation is that the children's friends and their parents will react in the same way, leaving the children vulnerable to ridicule and bullying.

It has been tricky at times to decide the best way forward. As a parent, you want to act with integrity and set a good example to your children, but you also want to protect them. For me, one of the hardest parts of parenting psychic children is the lack of guidance and parenting advice from anyone who understands our unique situation. It can feel lonely sometimes without anyone to confide in, and I've had to learn on my feet, as I don't always have the answers to their questions.

If your own children have psychic abilities, the decision about whether to share this knowledge openly with others is going to be different for each family, based on your specific situation. Our points of view, our parenting techniques, our beliefs, our environment, our support networks, our personalities and our children are all different.

I know with all my heart that being true to yourself is the way to a happy and fulfilling life. I am naturally a very open person, so the ideal situation for me personally would be to be open and honest with the people we meet, and admit to them the gifts the children have. However, the reality is, the effect of sharing this news could make life at school and in our small community very difficult for our family, especially the children. For now, we continue to protect the children by keeping their psychic medium abilities private, until they are old enough to decide when they are ready to share their gift with others.

I do believe that by sharing our stories we can all learn from and support each other. Having largely avoided social media and networking sites for many years, I unknowingly missed the opportunity to share and receive support from other families going through similar experiences. This realization has led to me creating a website www.raisingfaith.co.uk where you can share your story, so that together we can create a resource full of love, support and inspiration to help each other raise these extraordinary sensitive, empathic and psychic children.

GREAT GRANDDAD

Several years before the conversation with Tom's teacher, I was holding my children's hands as we walked across the supermarket car park to the café. Faith was five years old, and Tom was three.

Out of nowhere Tom suddenly announced excitedly, "Mummy, Great-granddad's walking with us!"

I glanced at Tom surprised. "Oh good grief, not you, too! You can see Great-granddad?" I was open-minded to the possibility, but thought it was most likely that Tom had just picked up on Faith and I occasionally talking about Great-granddad. Tom smiled up at me.

Faith looked up at me and said, "It's true, Mummy, Great-granddad is walking with us!"

I shifted my gaze to Faith with a surprised look. "Seriously?" I asked. Gloria had told me as much, but this was the first time Tom had volunteered information about spirit visitors. "Well, hi, Granddad," I said out loud, as we continued walking.

We reached the café and chose a table with four chairs around it. I threw our coats and bags onto the spare chair, to a fit of giggles from both the children. "Mummy, you've just thrown the coats on Great-granddad!" Tom said.

"Oh, sorry, Granddad," I apologized awkwardly. "Should I move them?"

"No, it's okay," Faith replied. "He can sit above them."

"Above them?"

"Yes," she answered.

My paternal grandfather, Tony, died shortly after Tom was born, and a good three years before we were walking into the supermarket café. Around the same time Tom was born, my granddad had become unwell. He only had one lung, having lost one to cancer 15 years earlier, and his health had deteriorated recently affecting his remaining lung. I took the children to see my grandparents when Tom was about 12 weeks old. I visited them frequently, but truth be told, I was still mastering the art of leaving the house with two small children, and so they hadn't yet met Tom.

As we walked in, my grandparents were full of smiles. Faith was particularly shy and quiet as my aunt and cousins were also visiting and she wasn't familiar with them. My granddad lit up when he saw us. "It's Tom!" he said, delighted that I'd bought the new baby to meet him.

My aunt and cousins suddenly sprung to life. "He's been talking about Tom. 'When's Tom coming?' he's been asking.'

"Yes, 'I need to see Tom,' he's been saying," said my aunt. "We wondered who he was talking about! We don't know a Tom!"

My granddad had been waiting to see my new baby, and looked very pleased to see us.

At the end of our visit Faith climbed up onto my granddad's lap to give him a hug and kiss goodbye. My aunt and cousins were open-mouthed with surprise. "She's actually going to kiss him," they whispered to each other. Despite how quiet and shy she was, Faith was very fond of her great-nan and great-granddad.

My granddad died a few days later, peacefully, in his bed at home, with my nan by his side. I've always wondered if perhaps he was waiting to see Tom before he was ready to leave. In those early days, the children would both tell me how Great-granddad read them stories at night. Even now, he continues to visit both the children and me most days.

A few years after Granddad Tony died, I was taking the children for one of our visits to see my paternal grandmother, Phyllis. In the car on the way to my nan's house, Faith was talking about Great-granddad and those stories he read to her and Tom at bedtime. I explained to Faith how much Great-nan would love to know that Great-granddad was still around, and she agreed it was okay to tell her.

During our visit, I told my nan how Granddad still visited Faith and her face lit up. She turned to her with a big smile and said, "Aren't you lucky!"

Faith looked up at my nan and smiled, then went straight to the cupboard between my grandparents' armchairs and took out the coloring books and crayons. She lay on the floor coloring pictures quietly.

Hoping to bring comfort to Nan, I asked Faith, "Can you tell Great-nan any more? Does Great-granddad ever visit her too?"

"Yes, he just came in," she said matter-of-factly. She continued coloring in her picture.

"How do you know he's here?" I asked. "You haven't looked up from your coloring book."

"I just heard the back door open, and he walked in. He's sitting in his chair."

I have learned over time that Faith 'knows' when someone is with us on many levels. She can feel them, see them in the room physically, see them in her head, hear them, and so on. As with other psychic-mediums, she has abilities beyond our usual range of senses.

Although I had never asked my nan about it previously, I knew that she used to talk about visiting the local spiritualist church, so I was now curious to know why and asked her. "Healing for my knees," she told me. Whilst I have learned that psychic and healing abilities can run in families, I had no idea anybody in my family knew much about spiritualist churches, psychics or mediums, but here my nan was clearly open-minded enough to visit them frequently for healing!

I asked her if she was ever aware of Granddad visiting her. "Oh yes, every night he's here," she replied. "The tea cups always start rattling in the kitchen, or my walking stick falls over by itself when he's nagging me to get up from my chair!"

My granddad was forever making cups of milky tea for my nan and their regular visitors, so it was no surprise to me that the tea cups rattling would be a good sign that he was home. Also, despite two hip operations my nan was not inclined to move much. She found the post-operative exercises too painful, and she far preferred to sit in her chair and have Granddad fetch and carry things to her instead of having to get up. She understood that when her walking stick fell over it was Granddad telling her to get up and move!

GREAT-NAN IS FLYING

My grandmother, Phyllis, died several years after Granddad Tony, her husband of 67 years. One afternoon when Tom had just turned five years old and had recently started school, my children had each invited a friend over for tea. I had agreed to drop the friends back at their homes afterwards.

I had already dropped Tom's friend at his house, and was just driving to the other side of our village to drop Faith's friend Catherine home when Tom announced to me excitedly, "Mummy, Great-nan is flying next to the car!"

You can imagine the confused look on Catherine's face!

"Okay, Tom, we'll talk about that in a minute," I said, grappling for the right words to delay the conversation until after we had dropped Faith's friend home.

"What do you mean? Who's flying next to the car? I can't see anyone," said a very confused Catherine, turning to look out the car windows in every direction.

Faith remained silent. I admit I drove a bit quicker at that point. I couldn't get Catherine home fast enough! I didn't want to lie to her, especially with both my young children listening to my every word! Equally, I didn't want to dismiss or discredit Tom's comments as nonsense either, as that was going to upset him. "Tom sometimes sees things we can't all see," I explained, hoping that would end the awkward conversation. I swiftly changed the subject to something else and I was able to drop Catherine home without any further mention of it.

Once it was just the three of us in the car, I was able to talk to Tom properly about what he had seen. "Okay, Tom, is Great-nan still with us?"

Tom squeezed his eyes tightly and then said, "Yes. She's here."

I looked to Faith for confirmation, and she nodded. "She's

sitting between me and Tom now, but she was outside the car when Tom said. She wasn't exactly flying. She was just moving alongside the car as we were driving along."

I tried to understand more about what Tom experienced. In addition to 'seeing' his great-nan flying next to the car, he often talked about symbols he could see when he closed his eyes. The shapes represented different people to Tom, and he could accurately identify who was visiting based on these shapes. On one occasion he told me that when he saw diamonds behind his closed eyes, he knew it was a man visiting, and circles meant it was a lady. This still didn't explain to me how he knew which spirit was visiting, and unfortunately he was too young to explain it any clearer to me, but Faith was able to confirm his accuracy on many occasions.

I am aware that some people with psychic abilities use rune stones with symbols on them. Different psychic people are drawn to the methods that work better for them. Some prefer to hold a possession that belonged to the deceased loved one whilst communicating with them in spirit; others prefer to hold colored ribbons or tarot cards; or to draw pictures on paper. There are many methods used by psychic people, and I suspect rune stones with symbols might work well for Tom too.

JOURNEY OF SPIRITUAL DEVELOPMENT

After my fascinating experience on the stage at the spiritual church, and with regular conversations with Faith and Tom about spirit visitors, my appetite for knowledge about spirit matters grew. I continued to educate myself as much as possible about the spirit world through books, workshops and conversations with other psychic mediums. It was important to me to learn as much as I could, so that I could answer the children's questions, but also understand what was happening, and how to keep them safe, should that be necessary.

I learned that being 'psychic' means you have an ability to tune into the energy of a person, place or thing. Psychic people can 'read' or 'feel' a person's energy to know past, present or future events in that person's life.

A Medium (or Psychic-Medium) can communicate directly with spirits, in addition to the ability to tune into energies. Therefore, Faith is a psychic-medium, as her main experiences are communicating with spirits. Faith's abilities include Clairvoyance (the ability to 'see' spirit people) and Clairaudience (the ability to 'hear' spirit people).

Gloria confirmed that I too had psychic gifts, in particular 'Clairsentience', which is the name given to people who can 'feel' or 'sense' energy from a person or place. I believe the gift of Clairsentience is common to many of us, particularly if you are a healer, carer, or empathetic person. You can 'feel' how another person is feeling, and often 'know' how to help them. Gloria described my psychic abilities like a flower bud that had yet to open, but with my growing awareness and interest in the spirit world and practice, I could develop my own skills.

In the first few months of my studies, Gloria generously agreed to visit my house regularly to answer my many questions, and bring something new each time for me to learn. One week she brought with her colored felt fabrics in red, orange, yellow, green, turquoise, purple and white. These symbolized the seven colors of the Chakras – the seven energy centers of the body which start with the Crown chakra on top of the head, followed by the Third Eye on the center of the forehead above the eyebrows, the Throat chakra, the Heart chakra, the Solar Plexus, the Sacra, and ending with the Root chakra at the base of the spine. Every color resonated a unique 'energy', and Gloria asked me to hold each colored felt in turn, and describe to her what I 'felt' about it. This was to help me learn to recognize that different energies affect us in different ways.

Another time, Gloria brought me used coffee mugs, and she encouraged me to try to tell her about the person who had drunk from the mug. I struggled. I had no idea what I was doing, or if I even had any ability at all, but I was willing to learn what I could. This method of communicating with spirit is called 'psychometry' and is used by some psychics as a way of 'connecting' to the spirit to whom the object previously belonged. All objects hold an 'energy' of the person who has touched the item, and it is this energy a psychic person tunes into.

Auras

Gloria explained to me that the colors we are naturally drawn to in our daily lives are often relevant to our aura at that time. Around our physical body, we have an energy field called an 'aura' which glows with different colors related to our chakras. The colors within our aura change regularly according to how we are feeling, and psychic people with the gift of clairvoyance (seeing intuitive information visually) can often see them.

Often there are several colors more dominant than others, and these tend to be the colors which we are frequently drawn to in clothing and home décor. I totally understood what Gloria meant about the colors to which we are drawn, and I think

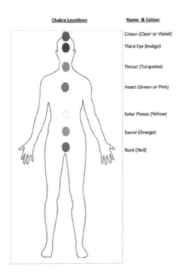

many of us can relate to this. Even before I knew anything about psychic energy, I often 'felt' what a room needed. I would 'feel' the colors which were right for the room, and even how the furniture needed to be arranged – much to my husband's frustration when I explained that a certain piece of furniture just didn't 'feel' right in that spot and he had to help move it elsewhere until I got it just right!

On a rare weekend away without the children, my husband and I were staying in Cornwall for a few days. We passed a shop with a sign advertising 'Aura Photographs' and in my curiosity to learn as much as I could about the spirit world and all things relevant, I went inside and had my photograph taken. It was a small shop with lots of spiritual items, books, ornaments, and crystals around the room.

Whilst I had my photograph taken, Paul wandered around the room looking at all the unusual items for sale. He held up a small black cauldron to show me, his eyes twinkling mischievously. I rolled my eyes skyward and turned back to listen to the instructions the photographer was giving me. I was asked to stand with a plain backdrop behind me. As I stood there nervously, the photographer explained that this system of photographing auras had been tested on hundreds of clairvoyants to ensure its accuracy.

My aura photo showed me surrounded by a blend of mostly blue, green and yellow bands of color. There were smaller patches of the other chakra colors in places, but those three colors dominated the photograph, blending like a painting around me.

When I returned home, I asked Faith if she could see colors around people. She confirmed she could, so I asked her what colors she could see around me. "Mostly green and blue, with some yellow," she answered.

"Wow," I thought. She can see auras too! I then showed Faith the photograph I'd had taken in Cornwall. Whilst I could have avoided paying £20 for that photograph, it was a wonderful example of how accurate her psychic abilities were. Sometimes when we are on holiday in a peaceful setting, like a beautiful walk alongside the river, or in the forests with the sun streaming through the tall branches, I will often wonder about the energy of the place. When asked, Faith will look around and tell me the colors she sees. Often, they are red or deep pink, green and blue.

Trust Your Own Instincts

I have read some fascinating spiritual books which answered so many of my questions and have been invaluable in helping me learn about the spirit world and, most importantly, have helped me decide for myself what 'feels right' to me personally. One of my favorite books is *Answers for an Enquiring Mind: Spiritual Teachings from White Feather* by Robert Goodwin. Among many lessons this book taught me, is that regardless of what someone tells me, what I have been raised to believe, or what a book says, it is very important to trust my own instincts. If it doesn't 'feel right' I discard that information. Maybe at a later time it will come to make sense to me, but maybe not. The most important thing is to only believe what 'feels' right to you deep down inside. I believe instinct is so important, and is the best way of judging the truth, whether it is a person, a situation or a piece of information.

It hasn't always been so easy for me to trust my own instincts. Having Faith living alongside me, with an ability to 'ask' for answers is all too tempting. There have been several occasions over the years when I've been anxious about which decision is best for our family or the children, and instead of trusting my own instincts, I have asked spirit for the answer through Faith. There have been many occasions when she has answered, "They can't tell you, you have to decide yourself," or they show her a speech bubble with the words "Trust your instincts," instead of answering my question. For important decisions, they are often willing to offer me some 'guidance', but they are very clear that I must choose for myself.

If we do not trust our own instincts and we instead follow others, or rely on someone else to choose for us, we are not learning and growing as much as we could. As with a child, there are some lessons which we cannot teach them, but which they must learn for themselves through experience.

Spiritual Workshops

To learn as much as possible, I attended various spiritual development workshops. These were held in a variety of places including village halls, hotels or spiritualist churches. One of these events was in a large village hall with wooden floors and windows along two long sides. Around the room there were small tables with two chairs. Once all the attendees for the day had arrived, the session began with a meditation guided by the psychic-medium running the workshop. This was to raise the energy within the room to help enable a good connection with spirit. The medium then walked around the attendees thoughtfully and one by one placed us at the tables around the room. We each sat facing a partner. At each table there was a different activity, designed to test and practice our skills for psychic ability or mediumship. Each time we moved tables, our partner changed, so that we knew nothing about the people to whom we were trying to pass messages. This ensured any messages we passed on were more credible than they would be from someone who already knew about your life.

At one table there were 'Rune' stones with symbols drawn or carved on them. Some people have an ability to predict messages based on the stones. I was to choose a selection of these stones from a black velvet bag, and my partner would attempt to give me a psychic message. Then we would swap roles. At another table, there were sheets of plain paper and coloring pencils. I recall sitting opposite a middle-aged lady and giggling about our next task. I felt foolish as I had no idea how to do this. I was to tune into the energy of this lady and then draw pictures of whatever came into my mind. I was doubtful that I could draw anything legible, let alone something relevant to her. I began drawing a little football player with a red t-shirt. Next, I drew a pie with hot smoke coming out of it, and I drew a Christmas tree. When I'd finished, and pushed the paper towards her laughing at my ridiculous drawings, she looked at me quite seriously and said, "I manage the under seven's football team for my town, and they do wear a red shirt." That stopped me laughing! I was stunned. She continued, "My profession is a baker, so I understand what the pie means."

"Seriously?" I asked her. "Pies?"

She confirmed she baked lots of things professionally, but yes pies were included. The Christmas tree was a little less convincing for me. She said it was her favorite time of year and she was known for loving Christmas and it was a big deal for her. On its own I wouldn't have thought this credible evidence for any ability, but overall I felt quite pleased. How had I drawn the young footballer and the pie out of nowhere?

At the next table I worked with tarot cards. We each had a

turn choosing a selection of cards, and our partner had to 'read' or interpret the cards for us. The message for us was inherent either in the intricate and colorful drawings on the card itself, or in the 'feeling' the partner received whilst holding the card.

At another of the tables I sat with a different partner and the aim was to try to give them a 'reading' – a psychic message or a message from the spirit world – without anything to help us. I sat opposite a middle-aged Australian lady with dark hair and smiling eyes whom I had not yet spoken to that day. As I sat there, I could picture a man in my head. I felt rather silly talking about a man I had just 'imagined'. He was overweight, middle aged, laid back nature, and seemed gentle and good natured. He was sitting in a chair, leaning right back with one ankle crossed and lying on the knee of the opposite leg. He kept holding his hands out to the sides, palms up. I couldn't hear his words, but it felt like he was telling me, "It's just how it is, go with the flow, nothing you can do to change it, it's all good."

As I described this man, the lady opposite me sat quietly with tears pouring down her face. We ran out of time to discuss who he was before we had to move onto the next table with a new partner, but at the end of the day she made a point of finding me. She took a photo of a man out of her handbag and showed me it. "That's amazing!" I told her excitedly. "He looks exactly the same as the man in my head!"

She nodded, smiling, and told me they had only been married a short while. It was the second marriage for both of them and they were very happy together. They had planned to spend the rest of their lives together when he was taken from her very suddenly by a heart attack. He had died within the last six months, and she was grieving for him. The message I had given this lady had brought her enormous comfort, and I was so delighted to have helped her, even though I wasn't sure how it had happened!

Gift of Touch

Over the past few years my senses have become more attuned to energies, and my own psychic gifts have increased. I have become aware of spirits 'touching' me to let me know they're with me. This first started with my paternal granddad. I was sitting quietly one Sunday afternoon and there was an obvious vibrating sensation on my head – like a repetitive gentle tapping but it was isolated to a specific area. I had noticed it on previous occasions but hadn't given it much thought before. It occurred to me to ask Faith if she could see anything around me and she looked up to my side and told me, "Great-granddad is here." On numerous occasions I would feel this same sensation and every time I asked Faith, it was always Great-granddad. As time went on, I gradually recognized new touch 'signals' and each time, without knowing which signal I was experiencing, Faith could consistently tell me which visitor was with me.

When I first started on my journey of learning about the spirit world, the idea of a spirit 'touching' me would have been terrifying, but after all these years of learning about spirit, and talking to Faith about our spirit visitors, I don't find their touch frightening at all, in fact I find it very comforting. I feel blessed that I am now able to identify which of my relatives is visiting me, watching how my life is progressing, and guiding me on my life journey.

Each of my spirit visitors has a unique touch-signal and therefore, when I feel a new 'touch' I know that somebody new is visiting me.

Some signals are stronger than others. Within busy or noisy environments, I find it easier to recognize the stronger signals, whereas the gentler signals from some spirit visitors, I mostly recognize when I'm in a quiet environment without other distractions. Occasionally, if one of my spirit visitors has something important to tell me, and Faith is nearby, they can be quite insistent with their signals. They only stop once I've asked

Faith what they want to tell me.

It is important to know that our deceased loved ones are often right by our side, helping us, and watching over us. They are fully aware of how our lives are progressing, even though their physical body has left this world. Whilst not everyone can see, hear or feel spirit visitors, we can talk to them anytime, they always hear us, and they will always be helping us. Look for the signs, for the coincidences that remind you of them, they will often be right there trying to get your attention.

If you would like to develop your own abilities, your local spiritualist church may run an 'open circle' evening where beginners and improvers are able to practice their skills. It was at one of these evenings that I first took part in an activity to help me recognize touch. During this evening we were put into pairs. One of the pair would sit on a chair with their eyes closed and their partner would stand some distance behind them. The one standing would gradually (and very quietly) move closer to the chair. The person sitting was to try to sense when their partner was close to them, at which point they would put their hand up to indicate this.

SPIRIT GUIDES

Through my research and personal experiences, I have learned that in addition to our loved ones who have passed on, there are other spirits helping us. They are known as our 'guides' or spirit helpers. Spirit people help us navigate through life to learn the lessons we require for our own personal growth. We are all on a different learning journey. Many of our biggest lessons come from the more challenging and painful experiences. These experiences often enable us to learn something important, prompt us to make changes in our lives, or perhaps reflect on how we might do things differently next time, contributing to our personal and spiritual growth.

Throughout these experiences, our guides are right there by our sides. They guide us on our pathway from one lesson to the next. They radiate unconditional love and acceptance of whom we choose to be. There is no judgment. Each of our guides has a different role. We have a main guide who has been with us since birth, and will always be with us until we leave this world. We also have other guides who come to help us with specific lessons. As we progress through life, new guides will come to help us learn new things and sometimes leave again once that lesson is complete.

Our guides are always there to help and guide us. We can talk to them at any time and they will be with us instantly. Even when they are not physically next to us, they can hear us and answer us. I learned from Gloria and my own spirit guides that, thankfully, spirit can also tune-out to the everyday conversations, which is fortunate for them, as some of us are quite chatty! If you ever need help or guidance just ask them, either out loud or in your head. They can always hear you. They will always be helping you.

Around the time I first started learning about the spirit world, my friend Gilly had an interesting experience with her guides. She was lying in the bath one night feeling disillusioned and alone. She was at a crossroads in her life and she didn't know which way to turn, and she really needed some help and guidance.

Whilst she had no experience with anything spiritual, she started a conversation in her head about how hard she was finding things, and the choices she needed to make. In the bathroom with her was a candelabra with six lit candles. She asked, "If there's someone here who can help me, please show me a sign." One of the candles went out immediately. Despite never having experienced anything like this before, she felt very safe and calm. She continued hesitantly asking the questions she needed answers to, and giving options for answers. Each time, at the appropriate option, another candle went out, giving her the answers she needed.

She rang me the next day, and as she told me, goose bumps sprang up all over my skin. She wasn't sure exactly how it happened, but she was amused by the whole experience. To know there was more in this world than meets the eye, that she was not alone, and always had help when she needed, brought her great comfort during a difficult period in her life.

I believe fear holds many people back from this type of experience. If your guides feel you are frightened of them, they will not show themselves, they will not alarm you. They will always help you when you ask, but they will only show themselves in a way that you are comfortable with.

Equally, our loved ones who have passed into spirit will often try to communicate with us to let us know they are okay and that they are happy and at peace now. As with my own grandmother, they can use a familiar scent, which takes us back to a memory of them, or often, as you are thinking of them, a song you know that was special to them starts playing on the radio, there are many ways your loved ones will use memory links that are unique to you and your relationship with them. We usually assume these events are just 'coincidences', but I've come to understand that coincidences are special signs for us on our life path, so I pay special attention to these. I have written more on this in the chapter 'Coincidences'.

WILL

During one of my visits to the spiritual development workshops when I first learned something about my own guides, the medium teaching told me I had a main guide who was a little Chinese man. He was a "tiny little man, very patient" she said.

In those early years, Faith told me that my main guide is called 'Will'. Sometimes known as a 'gatekeeper', his job is to keep me safe and control which spirits do and don't get to visit me. I didn't ask much about him at the time, but I always assumed he was the little patient Chinese man I'd been told about.

Recently, I was talking to Faith about Will. I talked about him being a little Chinese man and she looked up at me suddenly with astonishment, then burst into laughter. She turned to look across the room, and laughed even harder. Will was apparently amused at my description of him too.

"Why would you think he was a Chinese man?" she asked me, laughing.

"I'd been told that before by another medium. Who is he then?"

She looked at the corner of her bedroom where Will was now standing, and stopped to listen. Then she explained. "He says he worked as a shopkeeper, at a small corner shop in Devon. He drowned on a ship. He was trapped in a room under water and couldn't escape."

"Was this in a War?" I asked.

"Yes. World War One," she told me.

"Did I know Will in any other lifetime? Were we friends before?"

"No. You've not met him in a lifetime," she replied. "He's been your main guide since you were born."

Will has been consistently by my side through everything. He is instantly with me when I think, read or talk about anything spiritual, he is with me when I'm upset or anxious, when I'm unwell, when I'm working with my patients, when I'm managing a difficult conversation and, of course, whilst I write this book. He is by my side encouraging, supporting and guiding me through my life. My gift of touch enables me to recognize when Will arrives. Throughout every day he pays me regular visits. We all have a main guide like Will. Whether you can sense their presence or not, know that they are with you always, but most noticeably in your times of need.

Over the years, since first reading *Many Lives, Many Masters* the subject of reincarnation has arisen on numerous occasions, both when receiving messages from spirit, from the books I have read, or within the spiritual development workshops I have attended. Past life regression is a method of recalling past life memories using hypnosis or meditation. This can be a useful tool to help clear any limiting patterns of behavior (e.g. fear) in your current life which may stem from an experience in your past life. However, it is important to be aware that the very memory that could aid our healing, may not be the most comforting to learn of. Sometimes what is hidden may be better left that way, until we are ready to learn from it.

TSUNAMI

In the last year, I have been aware of a new spirit who visits me frequently. When I asked Faith who this spirit was, she looked to my side and told me there was a young man standing with me. He told Faith his name was Adam and he had come to help me.

"Help me with what?" I asked. "Is he a new guide?"

Faith relayed my question. "Yes. He's come to help you with friendships."

I asked her more about Adam. "How did he pass from his last life?"

Faith looked at my side and then repeated what she received from him. "Big Wave," she said. Then her eyebrows shot up as she recognized what she'd just said. "A tsunami!"

She was able to confirm Adam's passing during a tsunami. Adam also told her that he was not British, but he was from Europe. He was on holiday with a friend staying in one of the lower floors of a hotel (he was specific that it was not the ground floor) that was close to the beach. Both he and his friend were killed. They were 18 years old and studied together back home.

During that first visit from Adam, Faith and I asked details to establish which tsunami this was, however, on later trying to double check this fact for inclusion within this book, we were told by spirit that they could not tell us. We accept that there are times when spirit feels it is best not to share the details with us. I respect that the details of someone else's loved one passing are a private matter for his family, and that our spiritual gifts must be used with integrity.

"Then the greater the power that deigns to serve you, the more honour it demands of you."
—**Socrates**

Interestingly, in the months that followed this visit from Adam, there was an unexpected shift in my friendships. Some friendships began to drift naturally. Some friends moved to different parts of the country and even abroad. There were changes within the children's circle of friends which affected the friendships I had made around school life, and some of the less healthy ones I had been struggling with came to a head. Whilst these changes were unsettling and upsetting at times, I have absolute confidence it was a necessary part of my growth, and Adam was by my side guiding me through it all.

BOBBY

Several years ago, whilst sitting around the dining table with Faith and Tom, I was aware of an unfamiliar spirit who was insistently tapping on my head.

I turned to Faith. "Can you please tell me who is here? I'm not sure who it is," I asked her, rubbing my head.

She looked up and scanned the room behind me before her focus settled on a point between Tom and myself.

She raised her eyebrows in surprise as she answered, "There's a little sailor boy standing next to you."

"Oh! Who is he?" I asked, intrigued by this young visitor.

Faith paused to listen to his reply. I watched her concentrating on the same area next to me. "He says his name's Bobby. He's Tom's older brother, and he says that Tom's being bullied at school. He wants you to help him."

I glanced at Tom who was looking quite surprised himself. I certainly wasn't aware of any recent bullying.

"Tom, do you understand what Bobby is talking about?" I asked. Tom was now nine years old and at Junior School.

"I don't think so," Tom answered, looking puzzled. He had certainly experienced some emotional bullying with several boys at school, but not in recent weeks.

"Well, thank you, Bobby, for letting us know, and I'll certainly help Tom." I turned to Tom and smiled. "How lovely that you have an older brother looking after you." I took the opportunity to ask more about this little boy. "Was Bobby a sailor when he knew Tom?" I asked Faith.

I waited as she listened to Bobby's answer. "Yes, they were on a ship together," she replied. "They were both sailors but drowned."

Tom's eyebrows shot up and he naturally looked a little alarmed at this news. "It's okay, Tom." I hugged him and reassured him he was safe.

Not for the first time, I thought about how news like this affected my children. Largely the messages and interactions we have with spirit are comforting, but this was one of those occasions when the truth was harder to hear, especially when nine years old. Interestingly, Faith rarely recalls the information that spirit gives to us. Because the messages come 'through' her rather than 'from' her, she doesn't take on what she is told. She just repeats what she is given and then promptly moves on with her day. She may remember Bobby's visit because she was surprised to see a sailor boy standing there, but she's less likely to remember what he came to tell us.

I am not aware of any further visits by Bobby, but I am sure he continues to watch over Tom. In the months that followed, Tom did have repeated difficulties with several boys at school. Interestingly, although I had always prescribed occasional doses of a homeopathic remedy to 'boost' the children when needed, it was a remedy I gave him that I often used for bullying situations that was the catalyst to Tom's confidence growing considerably, enabling him to deal with any further difficulties at school. I have wondered since if this was what Bobby was trying to suggest to me.

COINCIDENCES

Our guides are also with us whilst we are learning new things, and often when we are working. We all have guides, and for those of us who are naturally empathetic, or are involved in caring for others – healers, practitioners, and so forth – we have guides who help us help others.

During a conversation with a reflexologist, the subject of mediumship and the spirit world came up. She admitted she was terrified of the subject, but told me a story of a client who visited her one time. The client was an elderly lady. At the end of her reflexology treatment, she told the reflexologist how much she had enjoyed her treatment, and added, "I found that man who sits behind you so relaxing and peaceful." The reflexologist was shocked to hear this because she worked alone! The elderly patient had most likely seen the practitioner's spirit guide who was there to help her whilst she worked.

As a professional homeopath, I have previously worked from home. At that time, I would see my patients in a consultation room at the front of the house. Within the room was a large sofa and on the opposite wall was my desk and a chair next to it where my patients sat. On several occasions when the children were younger, they would visit me between patient consultations, or at the end of my work day.

Following the conversation with the reflexologist, and soon after I had been told of Faith's psychic abilities, the next time the children came to see me at the end of my work session, I asked Faith if there were ever any other people with me when I worked. She looked me in the eye, but seemed shy and embarrassed, and nodded to confirm there were. I realized by her behavior that there must still be unfamiliar spirits in the room, so talking about them when they were nearby was uncomfortable for her (as it would be for any of us talking about people as if they weren't there!). I asked where they were.

She pointed to the big blue sofa behind me.

"How many of them are here?" I asked.

"Lots," she answered. She explained there were some sitting and some standing and they were wearing different clothing. Some wore long robes and some wore long dresses, though from many different eras. After more questions, she told me some of the spirit visitors were familiar to her but others were not. They included my guides who were there to help me with my work, my relatives who liked to watch me work, and others who were there to support the patients that I was treating. It was a busy room!

After many years of working as a homeopath, I am in no doubt my guides facilitate my consultations with patients. They arrange who comes to see me, they reschedule my diary when they can foresee a problem that I can't, and they send me patients who I can help, but also patients that can teach me something. There have been many extraordinary coincidences over the years and I have learned they are just signs from the universe that you are on the right path in life. Those coincidences are there to guide you, so I play close attention to them.

One such 'coincidence' was when a mother had booked a consultation with me for her young son. When I opened the door I momentarily froze with shock. There, standing before me with her young son, was the girl who had once bullied me throughout my secondary school years. The impact she had on me in my school days was significant and I had spent the last few years of school in fear. She would threaten me in school corridors, chase me home, throw eggs at me, spread rumors, threaten me with fights after school, and more. They were not happy years, and twenty years later, seeing this same girl on the doorstep of my home where I now raised my own young family was a shock.

I took a deep breath and snapped back into my professional mode. I politely invited her and her young son into my consultation room. I didn't mention our school days, and neither did she. We both had different surnames from marriage, and to this day, I'm not sure if she realized who I was. She had brought her son to me for treatment and that was my role.

I've no doubt her visit was not a coincidence. My experience as a practitioner combined with our consultation together enabled me to see her in a new light, and to see how people grow and evolve on their own life journey. It was an opportunity to interact with her respectfully without any of the hurt and hostilities of our childhood years together, and to draw a line under the past and to forgive. Above all, to be given an opportunity to help her young son, despite our past together, was really humbling. It once again reminded me that the universe has a broader plan for us all, and this experience was part of my life's lessons.

Another interesting connection to her transpired during her visit. As a child, one of the neighborhood children I grew up playing with was Simon. He lived a few doors down the road, was several years older than I was, and was a kind boy with a beautiful face and blond hair. My siblings and I often watched him ride up and down the road performing stunts on his BMX bike, and he was always very kind to my younger brother.

Tragically, Simon was killed in a car crash when he was in the final year of secondary school. As I recall, he was a passenger in a car driven by a friend who had recently learned to drive. I realized during my consultation with this lady, that her husband was the driver of that car.

I had often thought about that friend of Simon's who was driving and had always felt compassion for him, speculating about how hard it must have been growing up and moving on in his life with the history of that accident.

Some months before my consultation with this lady and her son, I attended a spiritual development workshop to learn more about the spirit world. During this workshop, I received a message from spirit telling me that Simon visited me regularly, and that he had been helping me for some years. Faith was able to confirm to me afterwards that Simon was involved in facilitating my consultation with this lady and her son. He was looking after us all.

COMMUNICATING WITH SPIRIT

It is often suggested that children can be more 'open' and 'sensitive' to an awareness of spirit visitors. I have heard it said many times that many children are born with psychic gifts, but if their families or those caring for them do not believe them, these gifts can become dormant without use.

If you suspect your children may be able to see, hear or talk to spirits, I encourage you to listen to them. Whilst it can be easy to dismiss their stories as part of their developing imagination, with an open mind you may find they regularly see or talk to loved ones who have passed into spirit.

Recently, I was settling down for a quiet evening after putting the children to bed and Tom came out of his room to find me. I rolled my eyes exasperated that he was back out of bed. He whispered to me that he thought there was somebody in his room. I assumed maybe he had seen something scary on TV and, keen to settle him back in bed, I walked him back trying to reassure him that he was quite safe and there was nobody in his room.

He stopped me saying firmly, "No, Mum, I mean a spirit person is in my room."

Tom hadn't talked about spirit for a while and, as with many children, I suspected his abilities might be lessening as he was busy growing and focusing on school.

"Oh, I see, well let's ask Faith if she'll help tell us who it is."

Faith gladly jumped out of bed again and followed us into Tom's room. Tom climbed into bed while Faith focused on the area at the end of his bed. Her face lit up with a big smile as she told us, "It's Granddad." She was referring to my father-in-law who had died unexpectedly two years earlier and whom the children missed and talked about often.

Instead of being frightened, Tom was immediately comforted

and smiled as he said, "I thought it might be."

I kissed Tom on the head as I settled him down to sleep again. "You can talk to Granddad either in your head, or out loud and he will hear you." Tom smiled contentedly.

I have no doubt he talked to his granddad that night, as he didn't get out of bed again.

The following night the same thing happened. When I asked Tom if he wanted Faith to check who the spirit was, he replied quite happily, "No it's okay, I know it's Granddad." Once again he settled back to sleep comforted to know his Granddad was with him.

Many people can 'sense' their deceased loved ones are close by, or have experienced their own 'extraordinary' moments when their deceased loved ones try to communicate with them. When my paternal grandfather passed from this world into spirit, my cousin saw a shadow walk across her living room at the exact moment he died. She immediately rang my grandparents' house to be given the news of our grandfather's passing. Our loved ones will always try to let us know they are with us, so watch out for the signs.

Animals are often more aware of spirit than we are. At the exact time my father-in-law died unexpectedly, our family dog began howling loudly as if he were in great pain. As I wasn't home, my neighbors let themselves into the house to comfort him. They were concerned because his howling was completely out of character. We had no idea until later that afternoon that the two events happened at the same time. I have no doubt that my dog knew my father-in-law had passed, and he was howling with grief.

Since moving to a new house, on several occasions I have noticed our dog sitting alert watching something in the room, with his head moving from one side to another. When I asked Faith about this, she smiled and told me we had inherited two spirit cats when we moved into the house. They visit the house sometimes, much to the dismay of our dog.

It is my understanding that animals are much more tuned into energies than many people are, so pets will often be staring up the stairs, or across the room at something or someone we can't see ourselves; often it will be a loved one visiting.

FAITH'S PERSPECTIVE

Faith's abilities to communicate with spirit people is extraordinary. I continue to be amazed at the different methods she has of communicating with them. Faith has contributed to this section to help others understand how she experiences her incredible gift.

How do spirits communicate with Faith?

There are several methods. Faith sees them in the room the same way she sees living people; they appear as a full person, in color. Sometimes she *sees* them as an image inside her head, instead of in the room. When they present in her head she says they often appear in black and white.

Other times, Faith *hears* them inside her head, so they don't always present themselves visually to her. She tells me that sometimes if I'm asking a quick question, she just hears or 'knows' the answer, so can pass that onto me immediately. Other times, if we are asking lots of questions, the spirit will present themselves visually in the room and stay for the duration of the conversation.

Sometimes, she sees what she calls 'speech bubbles' like a cloud in the room. Inside this speech bubble she will see answers written down for her to read. This is mostly when she is passing me a message involving a complicated or unusual name of someone or something. Spirit will write it down for her in the speech bubble so she can spell it out to me, instead of trying to repeat what she is hearing. On some occasions, she has struggled to read the message as it can be blurry or moving and she gets frustrated when this happens. She described this as follows:

"Some methods are harder than others, but usually if I don't understand the message the first time, they will try another way of

getting it through.

"Longer messages are often harder to read or hear because they can appear faint or distant like it's really windy or they are really far off."

What do spirits look like?

"Spirit people look like ordinary people, they are simply people who have left this life and moved on. Some wear unusual clothing like long robes and old-fashioned dresses, but usually to do with their lifestyle previously.

"I always see them as a full person. There is a slight glow to them and this can be useful in the dark, but it's not spooky at all."

Are spirits always around?

Our guides and loved ones who have passed into spirit can always hear us. Faith described this to me:

"I don't call for them very often. Only when I have a bad feeling or I just want someone to talk to, but they seem happy to talk and play with me. Most of the time they are already there.

"I think they know what I'm feeling and therefore are easy companions because they know when to leave me alone and what to say that won't hurt or upset me."

She added that when I am with her and we are talking about spirit, it's like the door to the spirit world swings wide open and they talk very fast, and repeat themselves trying to get messages to me. She finds the repetition of the messages frustrating, so we have recently discussed how she can let them know what she is experiencing to see if they can improve it.

Faith has learnt to manage them better in recent years. During one period, a few years ago, she was always tired and it transpired that spirit people were talking to her often, and waking her in the night to give her messages for her family.

I asked other psychic people I met for advice with this and, subsequently, Faith simply asked them to stop waking her, and they stopped.

She has also asked her main guide Jane to manage her spirit visitors, so she can get some rest. Faith says Jane has helped, but the improvement doesn't last for long. It soon gets busy again!

When do spirits communicate with Faith?

Spirit people communicate with Faith throughout every day. Sometimes, when we are together and I have a quick question for them, and if it is convenient for Faith to help me at that time, she will give me their answer during the daytime, but for longer questions we wait until bedtime. This ensures Faith has a normal day playing or at school, and it's also easier to communicate with spirit when the world around us is quieter.

When Faith is in a busy, noisy environment, spirit often communicate without appearing visually. Faith says it can be harder to tune into them visually when the room is busy, but she can still 'hear' them.

As I learnt from attending spiritual workshops, it is often helpful for a medium to sit quietly before working with spirit, to 'tune in' to them. The hectic pace we live our lives with noise, lights and technology everywhere can make it much harder to tune into spirit, so peace and quiet is important.

When we talk to spirit together in Faith's bedroom, they can be anywhere in the room, but if she's tucked into bed, they are usually standing around it. Whilst I cannot see them as Faith can, I do sometimes see faint lines like rays of light coming in at an angle to where she is looking. Faith says they arrive with this light and she calls it a 'glow'.

Does Faith find spirit people frightening?

Faith has never felt frightened of spirits. Even those she isn't familiar with.

She explains,

"Spirits have never frightened me. It's nice that children like Jane visit me to play with me often, and I like listening to their stories. My great-granddad comes occasionally to read me stories and we play games. Overall, it's something, if I had to choose, that I am proud of."

Does Faith ever pass messages to other people?

"Sometimes spirits ask me to pass messages to people nearby, but I don't get involved because I worry that that person won't believe me."

Spirits will use any opportunity to communicate messages to their loved ones. Spirits know that Faith is a medium and they will ask her to pass messages to others, however, she is still a child and not comfortable doing this, the way a practicing psychic-medium would do.

Does Faith see spirits in buildings, like ghosts?

"It seems wrong to call spirits a ghost just because they have passed on. Often I do see a spirit in a house. Usually only one and that person often looks quite dull and unhappy. I think they realize I can see them because they often give me knowing looks. However, I see more animals in houses than people."

Do spirit people answer all questions?

"Sometimes when we ask them questions they just say that they can't tell us yet, or that we have to find out ourselves."

Spirit answer a lot of our questions, but not all. We also try not to ask questions that would be inappropriate to know the answers to. To be given all the answers in advance of things in our life happening would be like fortune telling, and that is not the purpose of communicating with spirit. Sometimes if we are worried about someone or something they can give us some answers, but if there are lessons for us to learn, they cannot spoil the lesson. We must experience it and learn from it.

Do you talk to spirit with Faith every day?

No, not always. Whilst spirit is communicating with each of us in our own way every day, our time together is mostly the same as other mother and daughters with lots of conversations about all the usual things including schoolwork, friendships, family events, and so forth, and perhaps the odd mention of spirit here and there. Faith knows how wonderful I think her gift as a psychic-medium is, and she is usually happy to pass a message to me from spirit, but sometimes if she's not in the right mood, or is too busy, she will say so.

I have learned over the years it's important to respect Faith's wishes, and if she doesn't want to talk about spirit, I respect that. Likewise, my own guides respect that too. Faith tells me that unlike other spirits who try to pass messages through her, my guides don't bother her.

FAVOURITE DAY OUT

When they were younger, one of our annual treats for the children was to take them to a local theme park, which was perfect for younger children. They looked forward to this event every year. They would save up reward tokens we had given them for good behavior e.g. playing nicely together, sharing, thoughtfulness, using their manners, trying new foods, helping someone else. The tokens were actually green shiny marbles and each time they received one, they would place it in a jam jar they had each decorated with their names on. They then 'spent' these tokens on something they would like. It might be a day at the swimming pool, or the soft play center, but mostly they would save them up for their favorite day of fun at the theme park.

One year I was sitting next to Faith on the little rollercoaster. We were waiting for the carriages to fill up before the ride started. I asked Faith if there were ever spirits at theme parks like this. "Yes," she answered. I asked her if there were any spirits in the empty carriages in front of us. "No," is all she said, and gave no more information. Understandably, she didn't want to talk about spirit, she just wanted to enjoy the ride.

I assumed that was the end of the conversation, but a minute or so later when the ride started moving she turned to me and said, "Now there are." It took me a few seconds to realize what she was talking about. Over the noise of the ride she shouted, "They wait for the empty seats!" This made me smile. How lovely to think that spirit children (and adults) were still amongst us enjoying the rides when there were seats available!

Around the same time, whilst I was learning as much as I could about what she could see, I asked about the swings in our garden. She could often see spirit children enjoying playing with the equipment. This puzzled me. How could I not see the swings moving? She saw the same swings moving with spirit children on them, when to me they were perfectly still.

Frightening Visions

A friend of mine told me how her sister had always talked of spirits when she was a little girl. She would see spirit children playing in their garden, but my friend could never see them. Apparently, her sister would sometimes see unpleasant things. Once when the whole family was in the car driving somewhere, the sister looked out the window and asked their mother, "Why are all those people hanging from rope in the trees?" It used to frighten my friend terribly and their mother would have to ask her sister to stop talking about it.

It had never occurred to me that perhaps Faith saw unpleasant things. She seemed surprised when I asked her about it but, fortunately, she doesn't recall seeing anything like that herself. After learning this, I asked our spirit guides to protect us from seeing anything frightening, and I know that they will help with this, assuming it is for our highest good.

On another occasion, I recall my friend and fellow homeopath telling me about her son's recurrent nightmares. He would wake in the night absolutely adamant that there were scary people in his bedroom. Although she could not see them, she could feel the negativity and unease in his room. She was already aware of his sensitive and spiritual nature. He would become very upset at any unkindness towards others at school, and he refused to stand up for himself when others were unkind to him, as he didn't want to hurt anybody's feelings. A few years earlier he correctly predicted he was going to have a baby brother and he would be called Luke. There was no doubt in my friend's mind her son was sensitive to psychic energies.

So when her son thought people were in his bedroom she used every method she knew of to help clear the negative energy. She filled his room with healing crystals and angel figures, and she stood in his room sending Reiki healing energy into every corner. She also prescribed him a single dose of a homeopathic remedy, which she felt confident would ground him and stop him being so 'open' to other energies. These methods worked, and not only did the energy in his room feel much calmer and more positive, his nightmares didn't return.

If you or your children do see or experience frightening spirit visitors, there are some suggestions in the next chapter in the section 'Protecting Our Energy', which may help you. Additionally, within the section 'Are There 'Bad' Spirits?' I have also included my own frightening experience and how I sought the help of an experienced professional medium to help me manage it.

SENSITIVE TO OUR ENVIRONMENT

In my experience, both raising psychic children and as a homeopathic practitioner, I see time and again how intuitive individuals can be affected all too easily by the world around us, both physically and emotionally.

Many adults and children who are sensitive, empathetic, and caring towards other people are naturally intuitive to their feelings. We use our 'gut feeling' to judge people and situations. We can 'feel' when people around us are angry, sad, anxious, irritable, restless or tired.

Most of us will have experienced walking into a room and 'feeling' the 'tension', or meeting somebody who is smiling at us but we can't quite put our finger on why we aren't warming to them. This is our natural intuition sensing the 'energy' of those situations and people.

Energy is everywhere. Different people, places, rooms, buildings and such things as music, all have their own unique energy. Sensitive people, and especially psychic people, have heightened intuition, as if we have an internal radar, which is constantly switched on and picking up this energy. This intuition is a wonderful tool, alerting us to dangerous people and situations, and guiding us on our life's pathway, and I for one wouldn't be without it. However, being sensitive to the feelings of others can leave us wide open to absorbing their emotions, draining our own life force energy, which sometimes leads to illness.

It's not just people that can drain our energy, the places where we spend our time also resonate energy, and this can either make us feel better or feel worse in ourselves. Have you ever noticed the difference with how you feel inside an office building with few windows and bright fluorescent lights above you, compared to that lunchtime or after-school walk in the fresh air with trees, green park areas or countryside around you? It's not just the work that is making us feel tired, the energy of our environment affects our wellbeing too.

Food sensitivities affect many adults and children worldwide, but it is my belief that those with sensitive, empathetic, intuitive abilities are particularly susceptible. Unlike severe food allergies, which can be life threatening, a food sensitivity is known to cause mild to moderate physical symptoms usually affecting the skin, digestive and respiratory systems. I have found, from experience treating my own children and many others within my homeopathic practice, that in addition to the known physical symptoms and fatigue, food sensitivities also weaken the emotional balance of our health.

Protecting Our Energy

If the people and places that are around you affect you or your children, there are simple but effective methods that can really help protect your energy, to avoid this happening.

Where possible, if you know that certain people or places negatively affect your energy (or that of your children), the best solution is of course to avoid or limit the time spent with that energy. Where that is not possible, grounding and protection visualization techniques can be enormously helpful for adults and children. I recommend incorporating this into your morning routine, so you are protected before you leave your home, and consequently remember to do it every day.

The grounding and protection techniques will not reduce your intuitive abilities, but they will protect you from absorbing the negative energy.

Once you are familiar with this technique, you will fly through it quickly each morning, so that it only takes a minute of your time. You can also adapt the method to suit your own preferences.

Grounding – First, sit or stand quietly with your eyes closed and your feet on the floor. Breathe deeply and let go of any tension you may be carrying. Visualize beautiful silver roots uncurling from the soles of your feet, the roots are growing in length, and are stretching down deep into the earth, rooting you into the ground like a strong tree. Regardless of the storms that may come your way today, those roots will hold you firmly, safe and strong.

Protection – Second, with your eyes still closed, visualize being handed a beautiful long cloak with a hood. It can be any color, but if you like, it could have a sparkle to it so it shimmers in the light. Picture yourself putting on this beautiful garment. The cloak is long and covers your body all the way to the floor, the sleeves cover your arms and hands, the hood is large and covers your head leaving only your face on display, and there is a belt to fasten it securely around your body. Visualize this cloak as a protective barrier. Only positive light energy can access you through the cloak, and if you are carrying any negative energy, this can exit through the cloak, and no more can enter.

Finally, imagine a powerful bubble surrounding your cloaked body. There is a strong white light coming down from above into the bubble, filling it with positive energy that will protect you. Your bubble acts like another shield. Again only positive healing energy can pass into it while negative energy bounces off and cannot reach you. The white healing energy replaces the negative energy that you have brought in with you.

You are now ready for your day, strong and protected from negative forces.

As mentioned in the chapter before this, if you are having difficulty with visits from darker negative energies, it may be possible to help 'ground' yourself or your children using a homeopathic remedy. However, this should only be prescribed by a qualified homeopath to ensure that any reaction to the remedy is managed. Please be aware that whilst many homeopaths are open-minded about spiritual matters, these two subjects are entirely separate, so an interest in both does not automatically apply to all. It is worth asking if they feel they can help you with this, before booking an appointment.

Although we may not feel any different after using these techniques, Faith tells me that whilst we are grounding and protecting, she can see the colors in our auras moving around, making adjustments.

TIP: Faith has 'asked' her school shoes to always ground and protect her, so even if she forgets before she leaves the house, her school shoes are already helping her with this.

Crystals – These beautiful, shiny, colorful and powerful healing stones can be used for many purposes, including grounding, protection and healing. Intuitive children are often naturally drawn to crystals and will frequently correctly select the exact stones that they need to help them at that time. There are many crystals recommended for different aspects of grounding, protection and psychic attack including Labradorite, Black Tourmaline, Jasper and some Quartz. A crystal healer can help you with specific requirements and healing, however, there are some fantastic books on crystals including *Crystal Prescriptions* and *The Crystal Bible (Books 1 & 2)* by Judy Hall.

For many years I wore a clear quartz crystal pendant necklace which I learned was a good 'all round' helper. I had 'programmed' this necklace by asking it to keep me safe from negative energies, particularly during my work as a homeopath. At one of the spiritual workshops I attended, we were put into pairs and asked to give our partner an item we had with us, so this could be 'read' by them. This method is known as Psychometry. I handed my crystal pendant to the gentleman next to me. The second it touched his hand he recoiled and handed it back to me saying, "Protection!"

"Well...that's not all I use it for," I said, feeling embarrassed at the strength of his reaction to my necklace.

"That's what came to me as soon as I touched it," he said. "It protects you."

It was reassuring to realize the intention of my necklace was so powerful.

Cleansing – At the end of the day you can also 'wash' off any negative energies. I use several techniques.

In the shower, I visualize the water washing the negative energies from me and from the aura which surrounds me.

Another is that on a windy day, driving home with the windows down helps. I visualize the breeze cleansing me and my aura, clearing out any energies that don't belong there.

Another method I use after meeting someone I feel has negatively affected my energy, is to visualize cutting invisible cords connecting my body to theirs. These cords enable them to drain my life energy and control how I'm feeling. The longer those cords have been attached, the stronger and more 'root-like' they have become, so some will need a firm cut to sever the connection.

Reiki or Spiritual Healing – These are gentle but powerful methods of sending positive, healing, universal energy to people and places, usually through the hands, although not always. It is my understanding that this energy comes 'through' the healer rather than 'from' the healer. These methods can help all of us, including our sensitive, empathic and psychic children. If you are a parent, becoming a healer can be a helpful way to restore balance to your children who are easily affected by the energies of others. It can also be a helpful tool to maintain peaceful positive energy in your home, particularly if your children experience nightmares or frightening visions. There are various levels of training available for both of these methods of healing, but often the introductory courses can be completed within a few days, and will enable you to begin sending healing energy to yourself and your children.

Renewal time – Sensitive-intuitive people, especially children, often need time to recuperate each day. Their senses have been on overload and they need time out in a peaceful environment to recharge their batteries, without noise, company or technology around them. There are children's meditations or healing music that may help. Often just playing quietly in their room, or around nature is enough for them. Many sensitive-intuitive people have a love of nature and animals.

Before my children and I were consistently using the above methods to protect our energy, we would experience regular fluctuations in our energy levels and emotional wellbeing. We could visit a person or place feeling quite happy and full of energy, only to leave feeling exhausted, gloomy, even angry on occasions, without any understanding what had caused the change.

Some months ago, Tom was invited to a trampolining birthday party. The party took place in a huge warehouse-size building which was fitted with trampolines across the floors and walls and, at busy times, there were hundreds of children literally bouncing off the walls. Despite having a great time at the party, he came home full of anger and rage, which he couldn't understand. It took us a while to figure out what had caused the sudden personality change, and then we realized we had forgotten to ground and protect him before he went to the party. He had picked up energies from a busy Saturday morning in the trampoline center.

On another occasion, I drove Tom to a friend's kayaking party. It wasn't until I arrived that I discovered the venue was at a military training camp in the heart of Army-owned land. I stayed for the duration of the party as it was too far to drive home and back again. I felt uneasy the whole time. I wasn't sure if it was the woods or the gloomy water, but I couldn't wait to leave.

The children had a great time, but when I got home I still couldn't shake the feeling of unease and irritability. Faith had no idea where I had been but, as I walked into the kitchen at home, I asked her to check with spirit what was wrong with me. She looked up at me and simply said, "You picked up bad energies from wherever you went. You didn't ground yourself." Of course! I'd just spent three hours at an Army training camp. I had no idea what might have happened there, but I was confident it wasn't good.

I also often pick up negative energies from people and their moods. Recently I was travelling in a car with a friend who was angry and upset. I was with them for several hours, but within about 30 minutes I felt full of anger myself, which was quite out of character. A while after arriving back home Faith walked in and I mentioned I was feeling angry. Once again she told me, "You've picked up someone else's energy because you didn't ground yourself before you went out." Upon hearing this, I belatedly realized my friend was now feeling perfectly happy and calm. All her angst and anger had transferred to me because I had left myself 'open'.

Both my children and I now ground and protect ourselves daily before we leave the house, and this is something I would recommend if you, or your children, are sensitive to energies. We have certainly found it makes a big difference to us.

Are There 'Bad' Spirits?

As a mother, since the first time I learned of my children's psychic abilities, I have felt anxious about whom exactly it is they are interacting with. Are these spirits friendly? Can they hurt my children? Do I need to worry about any of these spirits? How can I protect my children? I would like to stress that neither of my children have ever seen any frightening spirits, and they both feel perfectly safe with the spirit people with whom they interact.

I hold my hands up and admit that I had never wanted to believe that such a thing as 'bad' spirits or 'dark' energies existed, largely because the idea was so frightening, and partly because it just sounded so far-fetched! I'm sorry to say, I have been proved wrong. In recent years, I personally have experienced one situation that I would like to share with you, because I believe that by sharing our experiences we can all learn from each other. I believe this situation happened to me for a combination of reasons. First, because my work involves listening to lots of negative emotions during consultations. Second, because of my deep desire to help as many people as possible. Third, because of a lesson I had been ignoring, about protecting my energy.

In the early days of my journey learning about psychic matters I visited psychic-medium Stewart Keeys. He told me, "I don't know what therapy you offer, but they [my patients] are draining the life out of you, and you need to protect yourself better."

Foolishly I only half-heartedly followed this advice. Although I started wearing a clear quartz crystal necklace, and visualizing protecting my energy, I wasn't consistent, and often forgot completely. None of the other homeopaths I knew had needed to use grounding and protection techniques, so I naively assumed it wasn't necessary. Eventually my crystal necklace which I had become very attached to, shattered on the floor at my feet.

About two years after the advice I ignored, and some months after my necklace had shattered, a new patient visited me for homeopathy treatment. I could sense that straight away her energy was different to most of my usual patients. She was a very intense lady, very feisty, and during her first consultation she explained that she had threatened various other counsellors and therapists with taking them to court because she was unhappy with some aspect of his or her professional conduct, so I didn't need to be psychic to be wary of her. Despite this lady's intimidating energy, I wanted to help her.

Her treatment began positively. She responded well to homeopathy treatments with me, however, she was contacting me very frequently – sometimes daily – with pages of emails wanting responses to her many concerns and questions. Instead of reminding this lady to wait for her next consultation, I became embroiled in responding to these daily essays from her. Sometimes as healers, we so badly want to help others we forget to look after ourselves first. Eventually despite my best efforts, I realized I couldn't manage this patient, and it was time to stop trying. My patient/practitioner boundaries were weak, and I became exhausted, and felt quite ill.

Some months later I was still 'just not feeling right'. I had totally lost my sparkle and I felt gloomy and was tired all the time. Usually when I was worn down, I could treat myself with homeopathic medicine and I'd bounce back to my usual self, but I seemed to keep slipping back into the gloom each time I tried. I didn't know what to do to help myself.

I had asked Faith a few times during those months if there was any advice my spirit guides could pass on to me. I was told no and that I had to find out for myself.

One day I was so exhausted that I was hoping she could give me a quick answer. I was told again, "They can't tell you, you have to find out yourself."

This made me tired and irritable. "Great, that's really helpful," I retorted.

"Well, is there anything different about my aura lately?" I

asked her desperately, clutching at straws. Faith concentrated on the area around my body, then explained it had the usual colors, but there was a 'grey' around them, the colors were therefore muted. I began to think perhaps I was sick and there was something seriously wrong with my health, even though I had no symptoms to speak of except the tiredness and 'just not feeling right'.

Eventually, disillusioned with how I was feeling, and desperate for answers, I booked to see Stewart Keeys again, the psychic-medium I had visited some years before. In the eight years since I have learned of Faith's ability I have seen a professional medium twice and this was one of those occasions.

I had been sitting with Stewart for about five minutes when he glanced up at me, then looked away quickly. I could sense something wasn't right. "Do you do some kind of therapy that involves listening to other people's woes?" he asked.

"Yes, I do," I replied. Feeling the energy changing in the room, and I suddenly felt anxious, but didn't know why.

"I think you've picked up something along the way. I just saw it flash alongside you and then it was hidden again. It's right over your shoulder and buried into your heart chakra."

I froze, unsure what to do. I felt a mixture of fear, astonishment and panic at those words. I was never sure what to think when people talked about 'evil' or 'bad' spirits. I never liked the idea of labelling anyone with those names, but to be told something was 'attached' to me was alarming.

"It's okay. I've dealt with this kind of thing before and I'll sort it out before you leave," he said. I knew he had worked on television as a psychic, and was sometimes asked to clear spirits from houses, so I was grateful that I was in the right place!

He started to continue our previous conversation, but then interrupted himself sharply with "No, sorry, change of plan. My guide is telling me I have to deal with it right now, it can't wait." Once again, I felt my fear rising at the urgency in his voice. He took a dining chair from the corner of the room and placed it in the middle of his office and I sat myself on it. "It won't hurt at all," he said. "It's similar to receiving healing, so you might feel a burning sensation in your back."

Although his hand never touched me, I could indeed feel a strong burning in the middle of my back for some minutes, which was much stronger than the usual warmth from healing. I could also feel the energy – like an electric current running through me.

Once he had finished I sat back on the sofa, feeling anxious and concerned about whatever had been stuck in my heart chakra. When Stewart sat down he looked me squarely in the eye and then admitted that it was a very nasty energy that had attached itself to me. In fact, he said it was the nastiest energy he had ever removed, comparable only to an East African lady he had helped many years before who'd had voodoo inflicted on her.

At this news, I gasped. "I've been feeling unwell since treating a particular lady. She had also had voodoo inflicted on her!" I explained.

"Why did this happen? Why did it latch onto me?" I asked. "I had always thought energies attracted to like energies, so why did this dark energy latch onto me?"

"Because you're a light worker, a healer, and dark energies are always looking to wreak the most havoc they can. That dark energy can do more harm attached to you, with all the patients you see, than it can on one lady. You were easy prey because you hadn't protected yourself." Gulp. That was a huge wakeup call.

Immediately after that incident I began protecting myself, and as you can imagine, I haven't stopped since! I have always felt my crystal necklace shattered to help me learn the hard way that it is my responsibility to do what I can to protect myself from all unwanted energies. Our guides and crystals will indeed help, but we must first help ourselves.

Food Sensitivities

We know that the food we eat plays a crucial part in the nourishment, health, and functioning of our body, however, in those with 'sensitive' systems, even 'healthy' food can sometimes react negatively.

Within my family, as our sensitivity to spirit and energy has increased, so has our sensitivity to food. It took several years of recurrent physical symptoms before I realized my children were sensitive to certain foods, and likewise I later discovered I was too. I have since learned that having a food sensitivity can be common to those who are sensitive, empathetic or psychic. That is not to say everybody with a food sensitivity is psychic, but if your body is sensitive to psychic energy, then there's a strong likelihood you may be sensitive to foods too.

It is important to stress that I am referring to a food sensitivity, which is much less severe than a food allergy. Food sensitivities tend to cause mild to moderate symptoms affecting the skin, respiratory and digestive systems, whereas a food allergy can lead to severe and sometimes fatal reactions, e.g. anaphylactic reactions to peanuts.

As a proud 'foodie', having a food sensitivity was an unwanted bombshell that not even my beloved homeopathy could eliminate completely. Subsequently, I began a challenging journey of learning an entirely new way to feed my 'sensitive' family with healthy nutritious meals, eliminating the forbidden foods, to maximize our energy levels and wellbeing.

After recognizing the positive difference in my children and myself once we stopped eating the foods we were sensitive to, my interest in nutrition and food sensitivities flourished. I expanded my training and incorporated kinesiology treatment into my existing homeopathy practice. This is a simple method of testing for food sensitivities in both adults and children, which involves gentle muscle-testing techniques. Needless to say, this is after you have been examined by your family doctor and perhaps had tests to rule out anything more serious.

If you, or your children, are sensitive, empathetic or intuitive, I would encourage you to consider if any foods – even healthy foods – may be affecting your ability to stay in balanced health. Each person is so individual, it can be a 'light-bulb' moment when you discover the root cause of those nagging symptoms you've 'put up with' for a such a long time.

As a practitioner, the most common food-sensitivity related symptoms I see in patients are as follows:

- Recurrent infections (ear, nose, throat, urinary).
- Fatigue (physical or mental, e.g. brain fog or lack of ability to concentrate).
- Mood swings (especially 'anger' or 'controlling behavior' in children).
- Digestive complaints (reflux, heartburn, diarrhea, constipation, stomach/abdomen pain).
- Skin symptoms (dry, sore, cracked [eczema/psoriasis], pimples/pustules [acne]).
- Itching/tingling of the mouth/tongue/throat immediately after eating the suspect food.
- Aversion or dislike of the suspect food.

Although it can be frustrating at first to adjust our diet to avoid the foods that are negatively affecting our health, in my experience, the benefits are worth it. When our systems are so sensitive to the environment around us, awareness of the elements that weaken our system empowers us to take control of our own health, and make the choices that are right for us.

GEMS OF WISDOM

Since first learning of Faith's psychic-medium abilities, I originally set out to learn about the spirit world, but unbeknown to me, this was only the beginning of my journey. As time has gone on, more and more opportunities to learn have presented themselves, enabling me to understand so much more about the incredible universe in which we live. The wonderful gems of wisdom, which I am so grateful to have learnt from others along the way, have changed the way I live my life. This in turn, enables me to share the knowledge with my children, to help them embrace the wonders of their life, to understand and appreciate all their life experiences, and, ultimately, to help them achieve their full potential on their own life path.

Life Lessons

It is my understanding that our life's purpose is to learn from our experiences and choices. These are our life lessons. Some of these lessons are hard, but we often learn our most valuable lessons from the hardest and sometimes painful life experiences. These lessons give us the opportunity to grow spiritually, to become stronger, more evolved, more loving, more understanding, more compassionate, more forgiving.

The people who cross our path in life are often necessary to help us learn something important about ourselves. The most difficult people and situations we have dealt with often shine a light onto an area of our own development that needs work. How do they make us feel? Why do they make us feel that way? What element of ourselves is now glowing brightly like a beacon showing us the very aspect of ourselves that requires growth?

Have you ever noticed how some situations seem to recur in your life? Perhaps you often meet the same type of partner which leads to similar outcomes you've experienced before.* Or you always seem to end up working alongside a certain type of character that you struggle to deal with? Perhaps you have repeatedly found yourself in another financial crisis.

I have learned that when we have missed an opportunity for growth, or perhaps we weren't ready to confront the situation the first time around, the lesson has a knack of coming back to us again and again, until we have mastered whatever important lesson was hidden within that situation. Heartbreaking though this can seem at the time, the intention of the lesson is for our highest good, and the sooner we learn the lesson, the sooner it stops coming back to us.

As the saying goes, *"If you always do what you've always done, you will always get, what you've always got."*

We have to admit that unhappiness, painful experiences, and even obvious mistakes can teach us much.

Taken in the right way these same failures and discomforts can be the raw material of which understanding and will are made.

The reconstruction of one's life does not of necessity mean that such difficulties must be avoided.

On the contrary, it might imply that we face the difficulties that in his life we tend to avoid.

Rodney Collin
The Theory of Conscious Harmony

*There is an insightful book by Eva-Maria Zurhorst *Love Yourself, and It Doesn't Matter Who You Marry!* Which can help our understanding of *all* our relationships, not just the romantic ones. If you find yourself attracting certain types of people into your lives time and again, this wonderful book can help you understand what is happening, and empower you to change it.

When One Door Closes...

My personal spiritual development has led to my understanding that the overall route our life takes follows a pathway that was pre-planned before our birth. Before we were incarnated/born into our body, our soul made choices about the life we have come here to live, for the purpose of learning specific life lessons. Along our life pathway there are key landmarks which are the important life lessons we have come here to learn. Although we cannot change these landmarks, we have free will to make a variety of choices on the journey between these points.

As we make choices in our lifetime, the universe and our spirit guides help us to achieve our desires and intentions. As a visual person, I like to picture this as a doorway presenting itself with a new opportunity on the other side. We have free will whether to walk through that doorway and take that opportunity, or we can decline, and move on to the next doorway that presents itself. When one door closes, another one always opens. For most decisions in your life, you have a choice which doorway to take. Each doorway offers us different experiences and opportunities for learning, but eventually it will always reach the next key landmark in our life plan. This part is inevitable.

For those landmarks in our life that are important for us to experience and learn from, the same doorway we've walked past on several occasions may keep presenting itself to us. If we continue to avoid that important doorway, the choice of alternative doors will become fewer and fewer until sooner or later, we have to walk through that door. This is the part of our life that is pre-planned and keeps us following the route of our life plan.

It's important to remember we are never alone in this. Through the good times, and the difficult times, our spirit guides are always by our side, helping and guiding us. We can talk to them, and we can ask them for help. When you decide what you would like to achieve in your life, your spirit guides will do what they can to help you achieve those goals, assuming of course it doesn't conflict with your life plan.

The Law of Attraction

The universe is made up of energy. Every object, person, animal, plant and even our thoughts resonate with energy. Like a magnet, we can attract the things we are thinking about. If we are thinking positive thoughts, we can attract positive experiences, and this is also true for negative experiences. Of course, we cannot change the landmarks in our life plan, but in the areas between those key points where we have free will, we can attract our experiences according to how we are thinking and feeling. Have you ever noticed when you're having a bad day, you seem to attract more and more bad luck? Your alarm clock doesn't go off so you're late for work, you're feeling stressed and grumpy, and then you miss the bus. You finally arrive only to spill your coffee down your suit, and the day seems to continue going from bad to worse. This is a reflection of the energy that we are emitting. If you want to change the day you're having, you must lift your energy and think positive thoughts. Like a magnet, you will then attract positive outcomes. There are multiple ways we can lift our energy: music is a powerful tool for some people, meditation, yoga, exercise, laughter and spending time with positive people can also help.

For me, personally, the law of attraction has been an incredibly valuable lesson to learn, and especially to share with my children. If my children come home from school after a bad day, or worrying about test results or any new experience in their lives, we talk about how the universe is a magnet. Children can feel empowered, during those difficult times, by writing down positive thoughts and ideas to attract the outcome they would like to happen. They may like to place these notes under their pillow or in a 'magic' tin where they can keep notes of all their wishes and dreams. Assuming it is for their greater good, and doesn't interfere with their life plan, the universe will naturally respond to the energy of those thoughts and intentions.

Life After Death

From my research and confirmation from my spirit guides, it is my understanding that the 'person' we are today consists of a soul within a physical body. The physical body is the 'vehicle' our soul uses to live within during this lifetime. Death is simply the end of our soul's journey in that physical body.

The soul that exists within our physical body is only part of the whole. During each lifetime, the larger part of our soul remains within the spirit world, and this is known as our 'higher self'. Our 'higher self' contains the collective wisdom and teachings from all of our incarnations/lifetimes.

Robert and Amanda Goodwin's book *In the Presence of White Feather, Conversations with a Spirit Teacher* provides a deeper understanding and explanation of this subject.

During meditation or quiet contemplation, we can connect to our higher self. We can mull over ideas and concerns and find the answers within ourselves. Those answers come from our higher self, and from our spirit guides. Upon death of the physical body, the two parts of our soul re-join within the spirit world to become complete once again, thereby combining the collective knowledge from all our lifetimes.

It is important to understand that we each have a main spirit guide who is our 'gatekeeper'. Part of their role is to help protect us from unwanted energies, and this includes restricting unwanted spirit visitors. Should there be anyone who has harmed you in this lifetime, and has passed into spirit, they will only be permitted to visit you when you are ready to allow them to. It is important to understand that harmful acts, which may be committed by some, may be at odds with the higher self of that soul. As part of their learning and development they will in due course seek to make amends for their harmful behavior, but this can only happen when they are ready and willing. Forgiving those who have harmed us is one of the most generous gifts we can bestow but, of course, one of the most difficult. It can take many years, sometimes lifetimes, before we are ready to open our hearts and forgive those who have wronged us.

Therefore, when our loved ones die, it is only his or her physical body that is no longer living. The soul that lived within that body continues to live on. Once back in the spirit world, the soul continues to further its development, reflecting on the experiences of their lifetime in the physical body. The soul also continues to spend time with their loved ones who are still here in the physical world. Even though they are not in the physical world with us, they are watching over us, seeing how our lives develop, and helping us where they can. This is also true of our pets who have passed; where there has been a loving bond between pets and owners, they continue to visit us from the spirit world, bringing comfort and love to us as they always did.

Many people spend their lives grieving for the loss of their loved ones who have passed from this world. Their lives can be consumed by the pain and loss of being separated from them and the prospect of continuing their lives without them. Many people believe their loved ones are 'gone'. Some have little understanding or belief that their loved ones continue to be with them, that there is life after death.

This is a quote from the book I have recommended above *In the Presence of White Feather, Conversations with a Spirit Teacher* by Robert and Amanda Goodwin, which talks of our loved ones who have passed into spirit:

The one in my world is in the brightest of health and radiance. There is no sickness, there is no disease, there is no suffering, there is no regret. All is well and let me say that the one to whom you refer, who WAS and IS and EVER SHALL BE a part of you is happy and content and making progress in the realms of light as it was intended that he should. The sadness remains in your heart, but in his heart there is no sadness. The only sadness is that you are sad. When you place flowers on the spot and when you speak to the grave you are speaking to an empty place, for he is not there. He is with those in my world, with whom he shares an affinity and he is within you, in your heart and around you. This you must understand. Sadness is so prevalent where there is a passing, where there is distress but we must not hold onto that sadness forever. There is a time to be sad, there is a time to cry. There is a time to rejoice that the soul no longer has to encounter the harshness of the material world and the physical 'reality' but is set free in the realms of its true nature which is its home... where there is love, there is no separation. To you at times, there is a vast chasm between you and yet it is but a hair's breadth.

The Gift of Psychic-Mediumship

The ability of psychic-mediums to connect with our deceased loved ones, and act as a messenger between the spirit world and the physical world we continue to live in, is a precious gift.

Receiving a message from our loved ones through a psychic-medium can be a life-changing experience. After the loss of their loved ones, many people are stuck in their grief, or consumed with unresolved regrets, unable to move forwards on their life path. Receiving a message from their loved ones can be a catalyst to healing, bringing great comfort to discover they are still right here with us, and enabling us to move forward with our lives with new focus and direction.

Whilst some psychic people are gifted in their ability to 'tune-in' and 'read' our past, present and near-future lives, we should be mindful that learning about our future in advance can potentially short-cut the lessons we are due to learn from those experiences. As one psychic-medium taught me, "It's not about fortune telling, it's about bringing comfort to those who are grieving." I believe that psychic gifts must be used with integrity, for the highest good of that person.

After my maternal grandfather passed, my mother visited a psychic-medium. Shortly after she sat down, the psychic-medium was taken quite by surprise as she told my mother, "Oh, my goodness, your father is here and he's come in on a motorbike! He's whizzing around us making an awful noise! My goodness he does love his bikes, doesn't he!"

My grandfather did indeed love his motorbikes. He was often found pottering in his garage fixing and rebuilding motorbikes. He built a beautiful Triumph Thunderbird 500cc and we have a photo of my siblings and me as children sitting on it together.

My grandfather had died suddenly and unexpectedly from a heart attack. The messages and evidence the psychic-medium conveyed to my mother brought her comfort. To know my grandfather was still around in some form and had communicated via this lady, helped my mother process her grief and begin healing. He wasn't gone, he just wasn't with us in a physical body anymore.

THE JOURNEY SO FAR

I started this journey with the intention of learning as much as I could about psychic-mediums and the spirit world, so that I could understand what my daughter Faith was experiencing, and gain the knowledge to help her, if needed. My journey has become so much more than I ever expected, ultimately evolving into my own spiritual awakening. Whilst my newfound knowledge reflects only the tip of the iceberg, I feel my journey so far has helped me gain a deeper understanding of Faith's psychic-medium abilities, together with a humble appreciation of the universe around me, the reasons why things happen in our lives, and a growing understanding of my own life purpose.

If this book has found its way into your hands, know that there is a good reason for that. I hope that the contents within help answer your questions, bring you comfort, knowledge, and inspiration to help you progress forwards on your own life journey.

If you have lost loved ones, know that they are still with you, loving you, watching over you, and often trying to get your attention, so watch for the signs and coincidences throughout your life. Know that your loved ones are at peace now, and they can reflect on their life's experiences and see the bigger picture. Know that they want what is best for you, for you to move forwards and to live your life for your highest good.

If your family is blessed with psychic abilities, I hope this book helps you feel comforted to know that you are not alone. Raising psychic children feels like unchartered territory at times, and knowing where to turn for guidance and support can be overwhelming. It is my belief that by sharing our experiences we can all learn from and inspire each other.

If you have your own experiences with psychic children, I would love to hear from you via my website www.raisingfaith. co.uk.

RECOMMENDED READING

This is a list of some of the books which have helped me gain a deeper understanding of both the spirit world, the universe we live in, and the natural laws which govern the lives we have here in the physical world. I hope you find inspiration and understanding in these books. As always, trust your instinct and start with the book which you are drawn to most. We are all at different levels of learning. If the first book you choose doesn't make sense to you, that's okay. It may do at a later date. Start with the book that does make sense to you and gradually your knowledge and understanding will grow as you evolve on your own spiritual journey of learning.

Byrne, R – *The Secret*
Canfield, J, Hansen M.V, Newmark, A – *Chicken Soup for the Soul*
Goodwin, R – *The Golden Thread*
Goodwin, R & A – *In the Presence of White Feather*
Goodwin, R & Terrado, A – *Answers for an Enquiring Mind*
Hall, Judy – *Crystal Prescriptions*
Hall, Judy – *The Crystal Bible Vol 1*
Hall, Judy – *The Crystal Bible Vol 2*
Harrington, P – *The Secret to Teen Power*
Hay, L – *You Can Heal Your Life*
Newcomb, J – *Angels Watching Over Me*
Redfield, J – *The Celestine Prophecy*
Virtue, D – *The Care and Feeding of Indigo Children*
Walsch, N.D – *Conversations With God*
Weiss, B – *Many Lives, Many Masters*
Weiss, B – *Messages from the Masters*
Zurhorst, E – *Love Yourself...and It Doesn't Matter Who You Marry!*

6th Books

ALL THINGS PARANORMAL

Investigations, explanations and deliberations on the paranormal, supernatural, explainable or unexplainable. 6th Books seeks to give answers while nourishing the soul: whether making use of the scientific model or anecdotal and fun, but always beautifully written.

Titles cover everything within parapsychology: how to, lifestyles, alternative medicine, beliefs, myths and theories.

If you have enjoyed this book, why not tell other readers by posting a review on your preferred book site? Recent bestsellers from 6th Books are:

The Afterlife Unveiled
What the Dead Are Telling us About Their World!
Stafford Betty
What happens after we die? Spirits speaking through mediums know, and they want us to know. This book unveils their world...
Paperback: 978-1-84694-496-3 ebook: 978-1-84694-926-5

Spirit Release
Sue Allen
A guide to psychic attack, curses, witchcraft, spirit attachment, possession, soul retrieval, haunting, deliverance, exorcism and more, as taught at the College of Psychic Studies.
Paperback: 978-1-84694-033-0 ebook: 978-1-84694-651-6

I'm Still With You
True Stories of Healing Grief Through Spirit Communication
Carole J. Obley
A series of after-death spirit communications which uplift, comfort
and heal, and show how love helps us grieve.
Paperback: 978-1-84694-107-8 ebook: 978-1-84694-639-4

Less Incomplete
A Guide to Experiencing the Human Condition Beyond the
Physical Body
Sandie Gustus
Based on 40 years of scientific research, this book is a dynamic
guide to understanding life beyond the physical body.
Paperback: 978-1-84694-351-5 ebook: 978-1-84694-892-3

Advanced Psychic Development
Becky Walsh
Learn how to practise as a professional, contemporary spiritual
medium.
Paperback: 978-1-84694-062-0 ebook: 978-1-78099-941-8

Astral Projection Made Easy
Overcoming the Fear of Death
Stephanie June Sorrell
From the popular Made Easy series, *Astral Projection Made Easy*
helps to eliminate the fear of death, through discussion of life be-
yond the physical body.
Paperback: 978-1-84694-611-0 ebook: 978-1-78099-225-9

The Miracle Workers Handbook
Seven Levels of Power and Manifestation of the Virgin Mary
Sherrie Dillard
Learn how to invoke the Virgin Mary's presence, communicate
with her, receive her grace and miracles and become a miracle
worker.
Paperback: 978-1-84694-920-3 ebook: 978-1-84694-921-0

Divine Guidance
The Answers You Need to Make Miracles
Stephanie J. King
Ask any question and the answer will be presented, like a direct
line to higher realms... *Divine Guidance* helps you to regain
control over your own journey through life.
Paperback: 978-1-78099-794-0 ebook: 978-1-78099-793-3

The End of Death
How Near-Death Experiences Prove the Afterlife
Admir Serrano
A compelling examination of the phenomena of Near-Death
Experiences.
Paperback: 978-1-78279-233-8 ebook: 978-1-78279-232-1

The Psychic & Spiritual Awareness Manual
A Guide to DIY Enlightenment
Kevin West
Discover practical ways of empowering yourself by unlocking
your psychic awareness, through the Spiritualist and New Age
approach.
Paperback: 978-1-78279-397-7 ebook: 978-1-78279-396-0

An Angels' Guide to Working with the Power of Light
Laura Newbury
Discovering her ability to communicate with angels, Laura Newbury records her inspirational messages of guidance and answers to universal questions.
Paperback: 978-1-84694-908-1 ebook: 978-1-84694-909-8

Blissfully Dead
Life Lessons from the Other Side
Melita Harvey
The spirit of Janelle, a former actress, takes the reader on a fascinating and insightful journey from the mind to the heart.
Paperback: 978-1-78535-078-8 ebook: 978-1-78535-079-5

Does It Rain in Other Dimensions?
A True Story of Alien Encounters
Mike Oram
We have neighbors in the universe. This book describes one man's experience of communicating with other-dimensional and extra-terrestrial beings over a 50-year period.
Paperback: 978-1-84694-054-5

Readers of ebooks can buy or view any of these bestsellers by clicking on the live link in the title. Most titles are published in paperback and as an ebook. Paperbacks are available in traditional bookshops. Both print and ebook formats are available online.
Find more titles and sign up to our readers' newsletter at http://www.johnhuntpublishing.com/mind-body-spirit.
Follow us on Facebook at https://www.facebook.com/OBooks and Twitter at https://twitter.com/obooks.